Western Art for the Naive Art Lover

By

Lynne Pickering

ISBN 9781092791229

ISBN

This is a work of fiction. Names characters, places and incidents either are the product of the authors imagination

Or are used fictitiously, and any resemblance to any actual persons. Living or dead, events ,or locales is entirely coincidental.

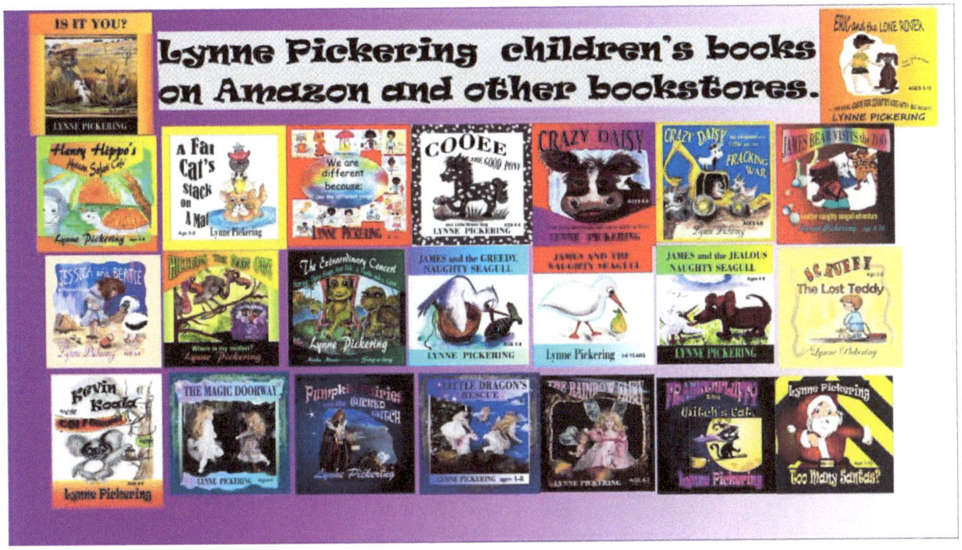
Lynne Pickering children's books on Amazon and other bookstores.
IS IT YOU?
Eric and the Lone Rover
Henry Hippo's
A Fat Cat's Stack On A Mat
We are different because:
COOEE THE GOOD PONY
CRAZY DAISY
JAMES BEAR VISITS the ZOO
JESSICA and BERTIE
The Extraordinary Concert
JAMES and the GREEDY, NAUGHTY SEAGULL
JAMES and the JEALOUS NAUGHTY SEAGULL
The Lost Teddy
Kevin Koala
THE MAGIC DOORWAY
LITTLE DRAGON'S RESCUE
Too Many Santas?
LYNNE PICKERING

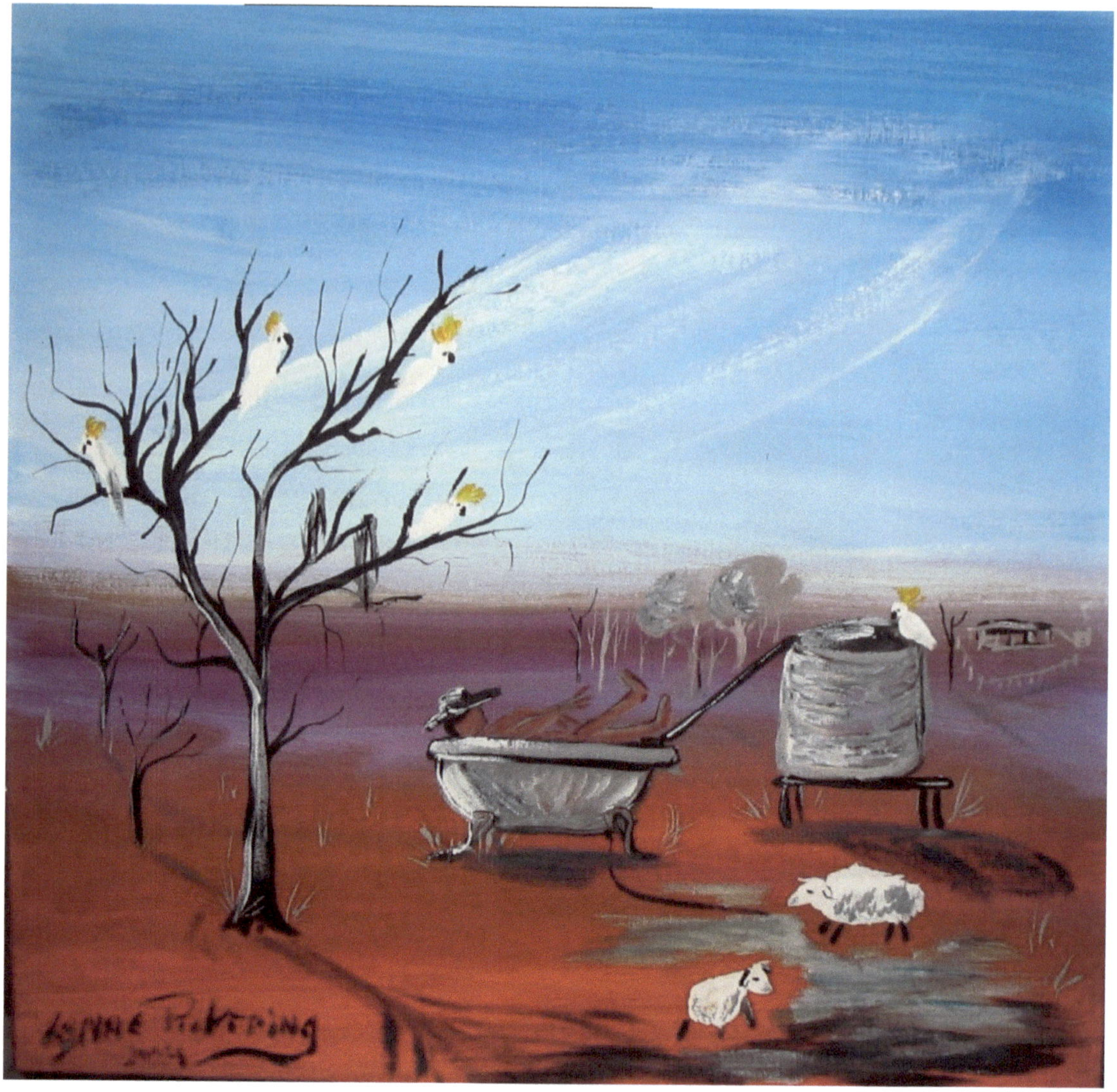

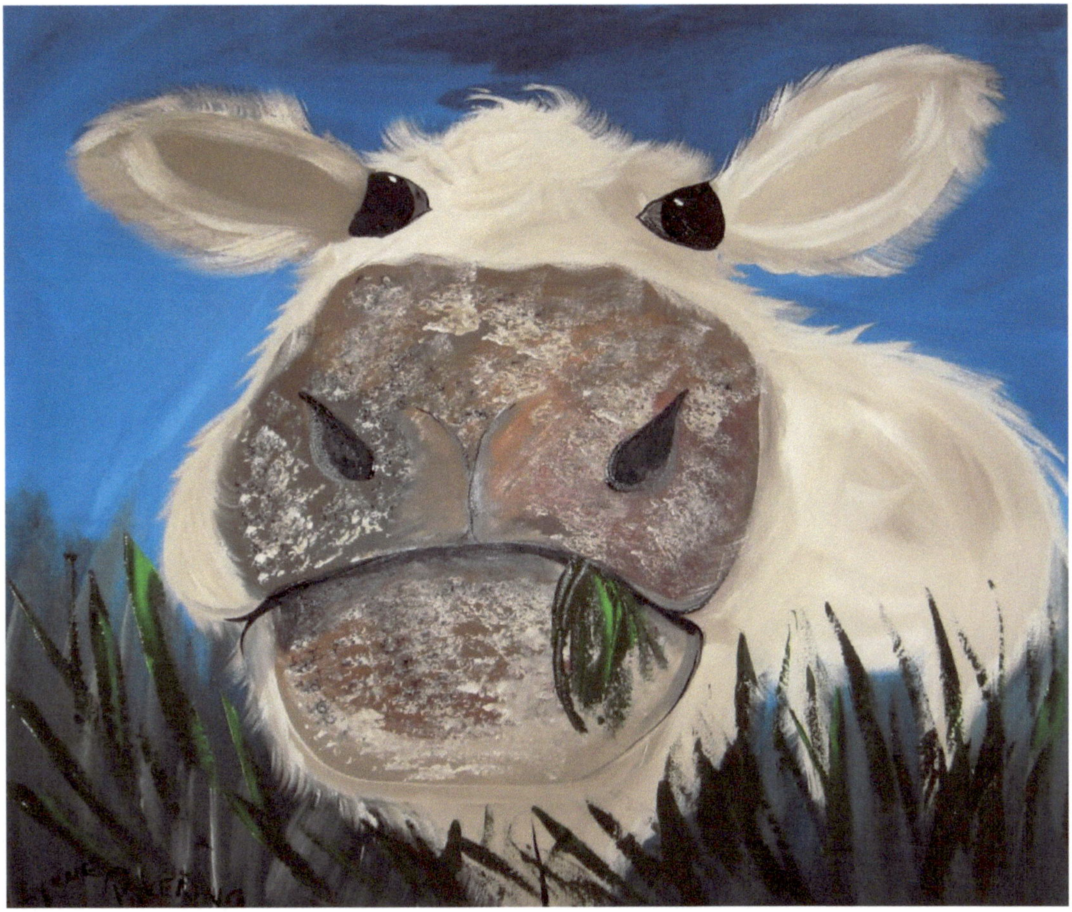

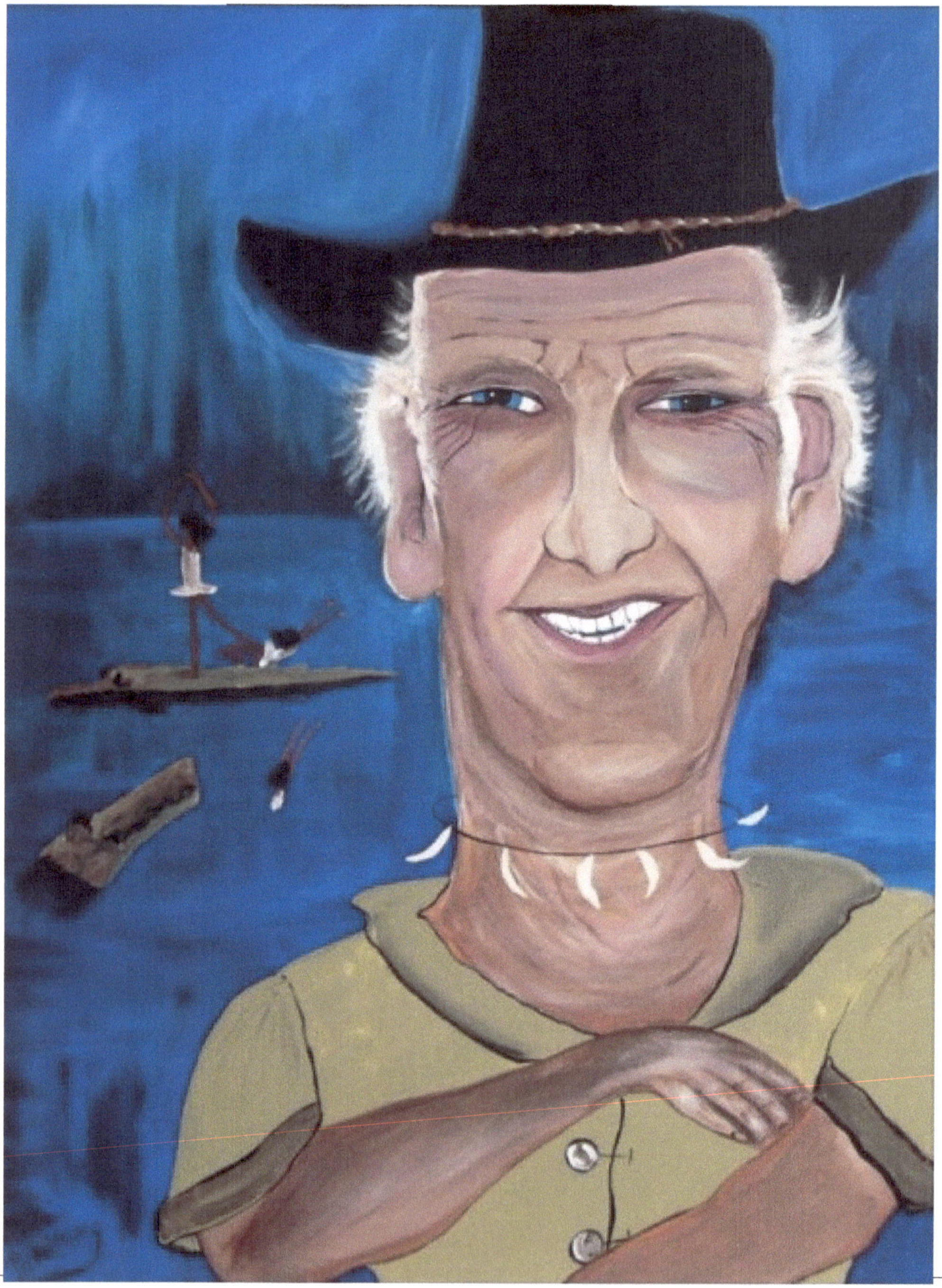

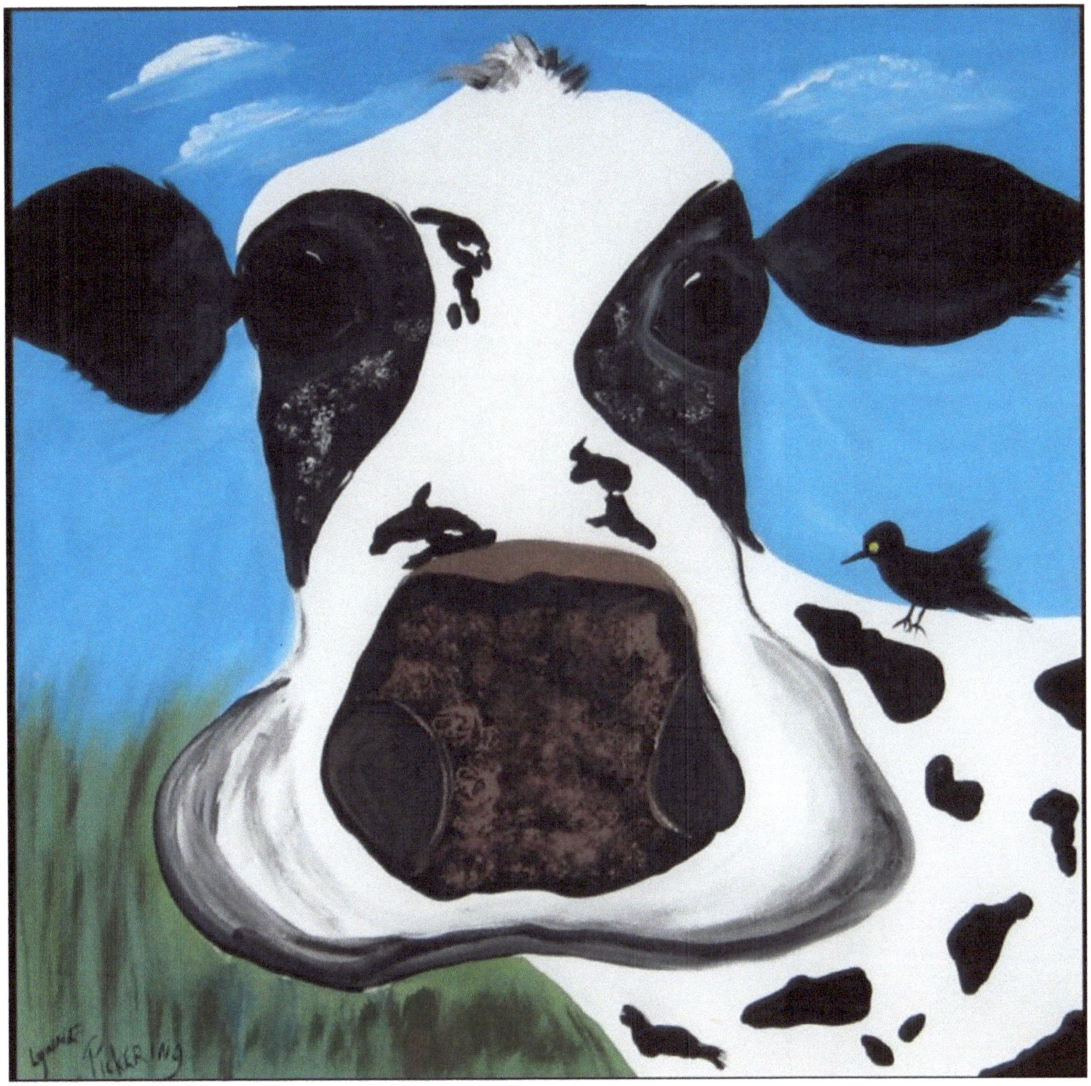

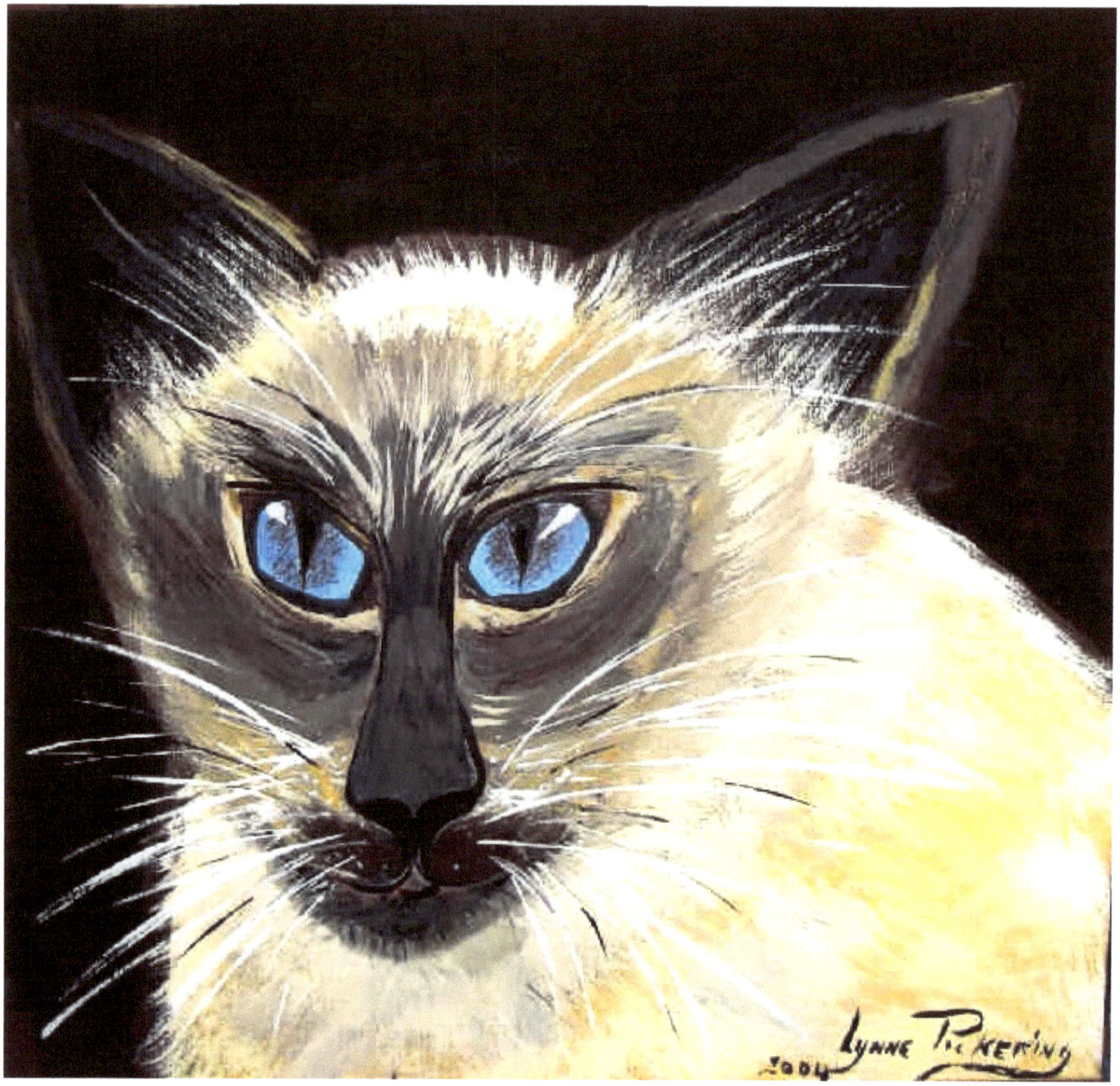
Lynne Pickering
2004

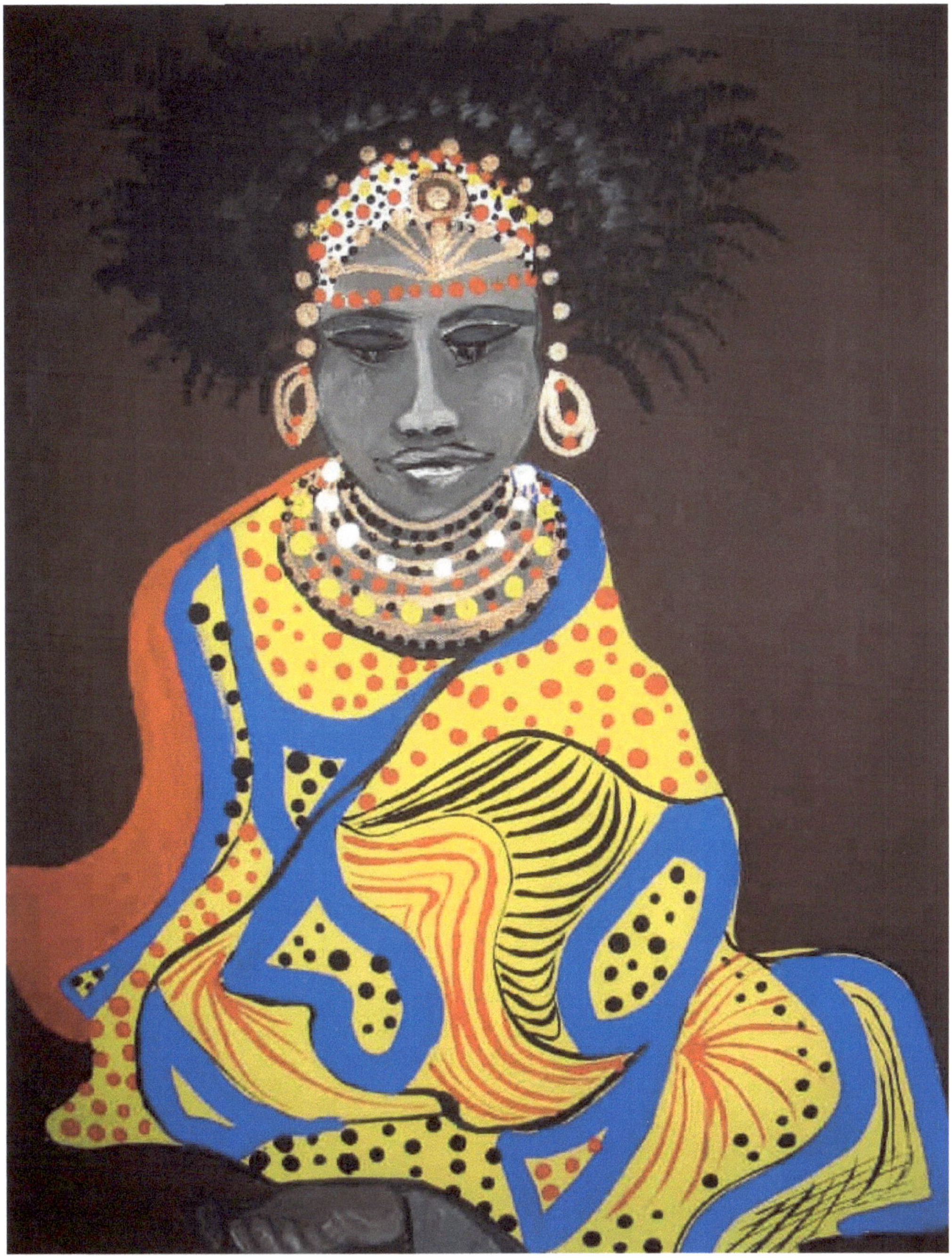

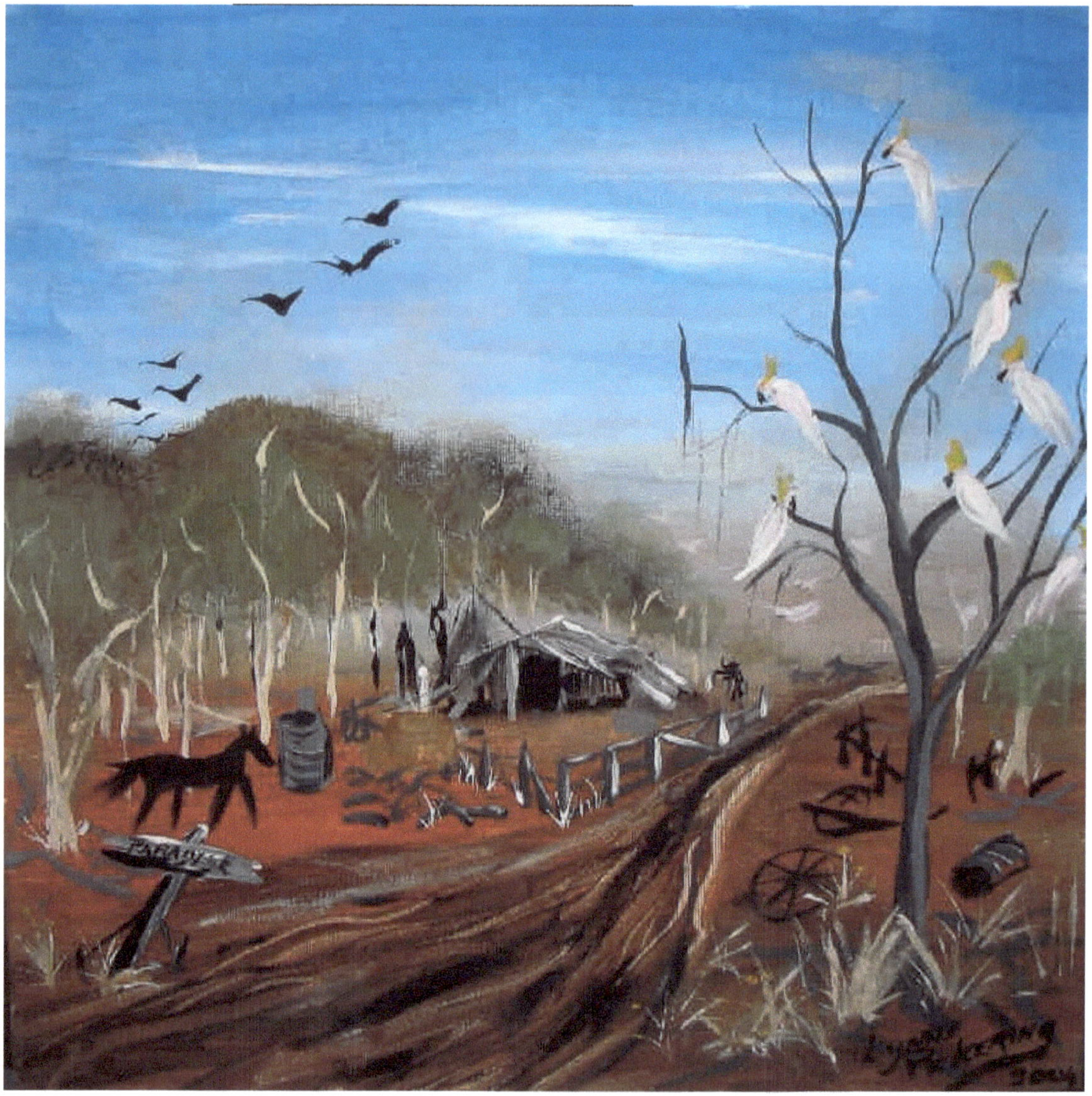

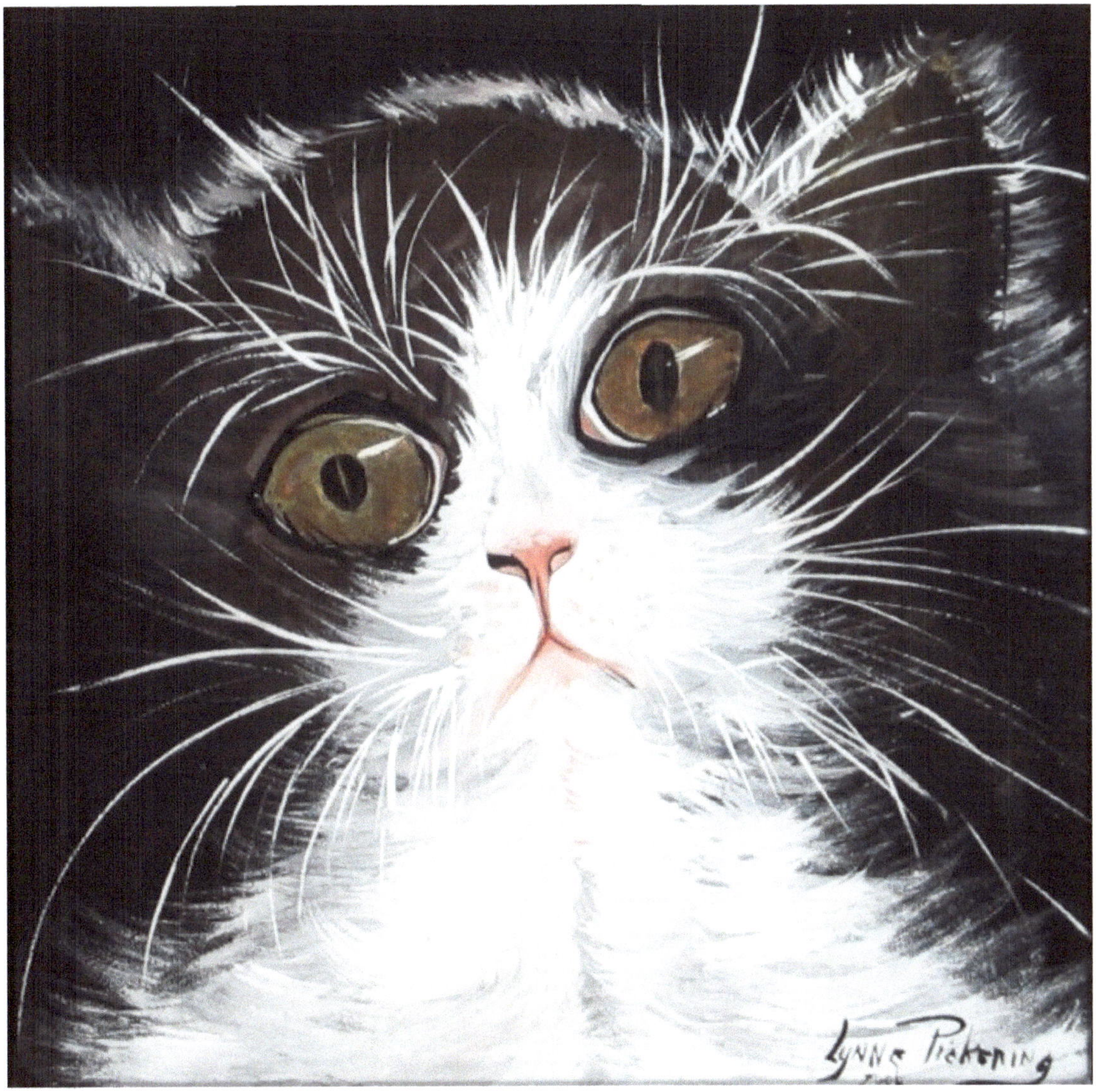
Lynne Pickering

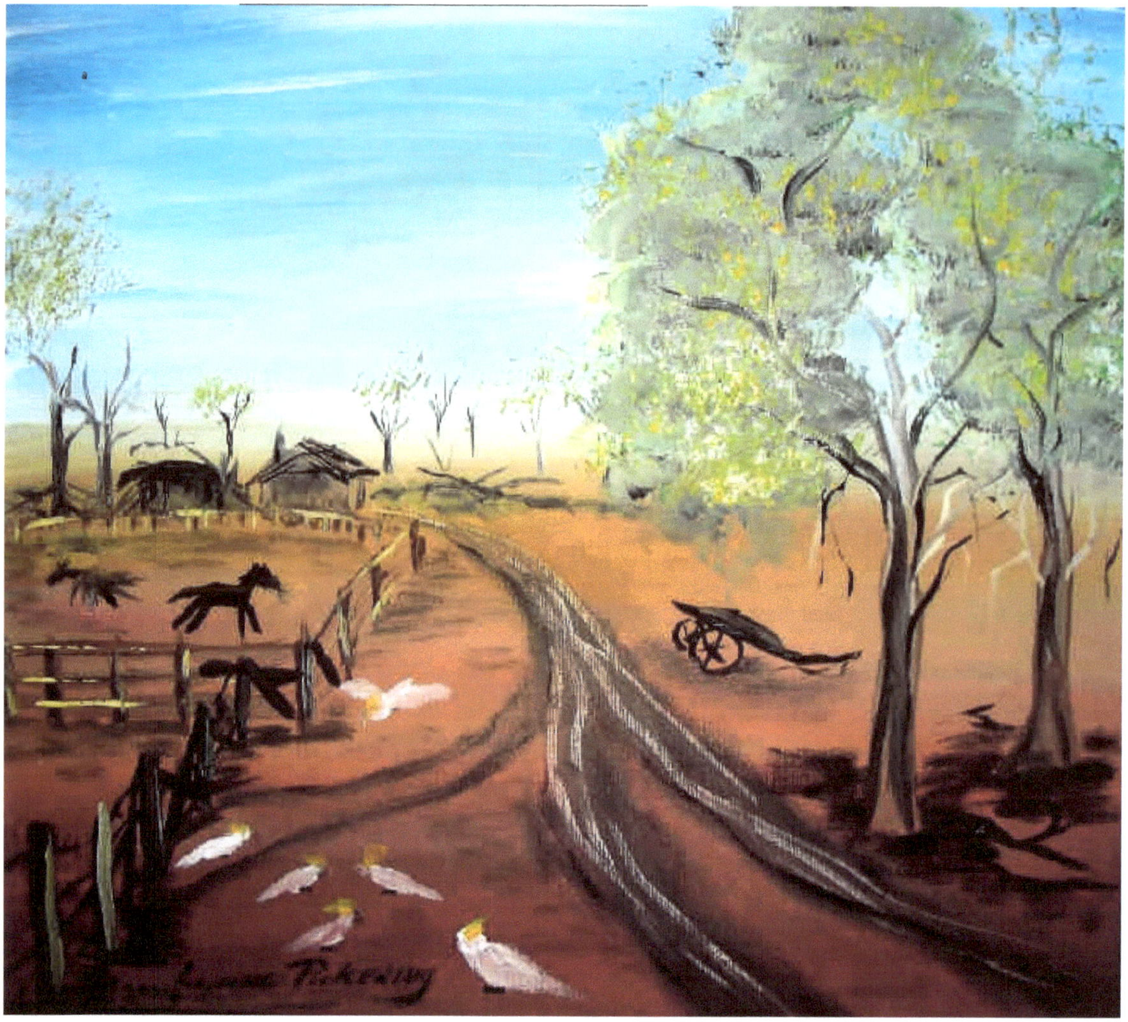
Lynne Pickering

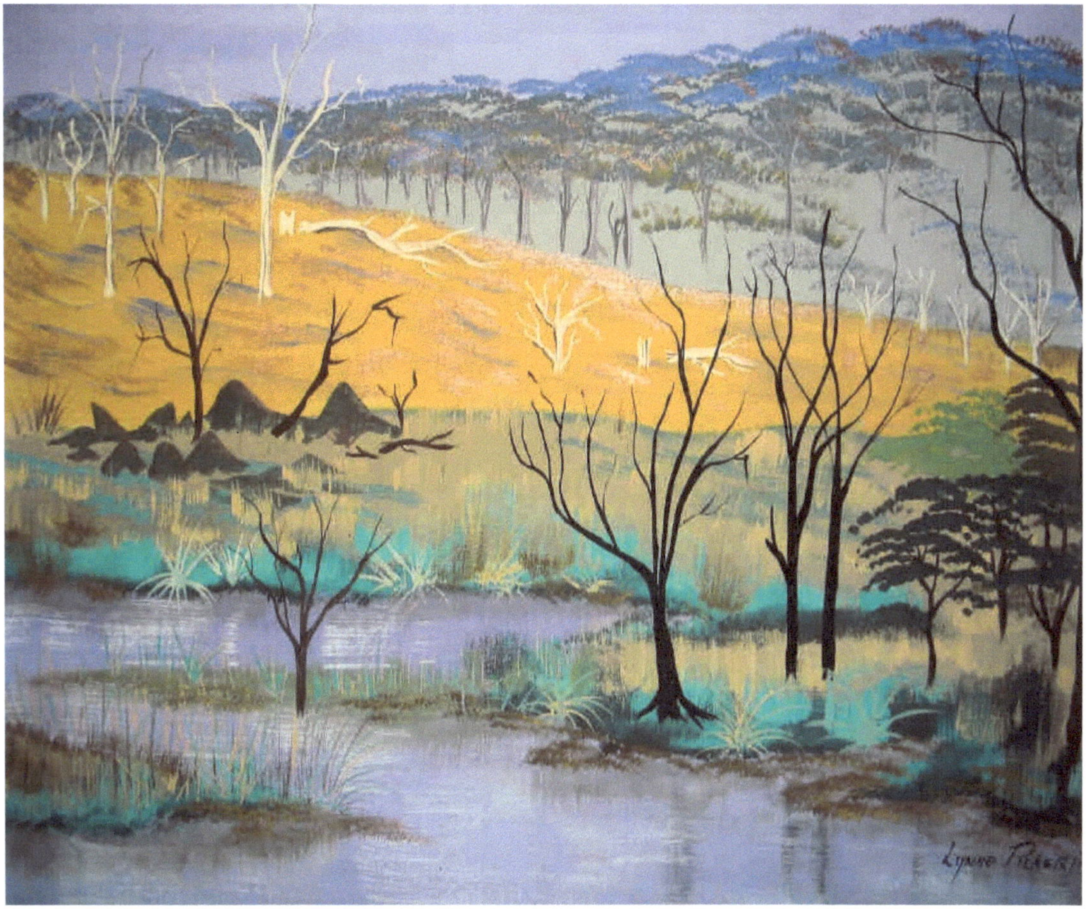

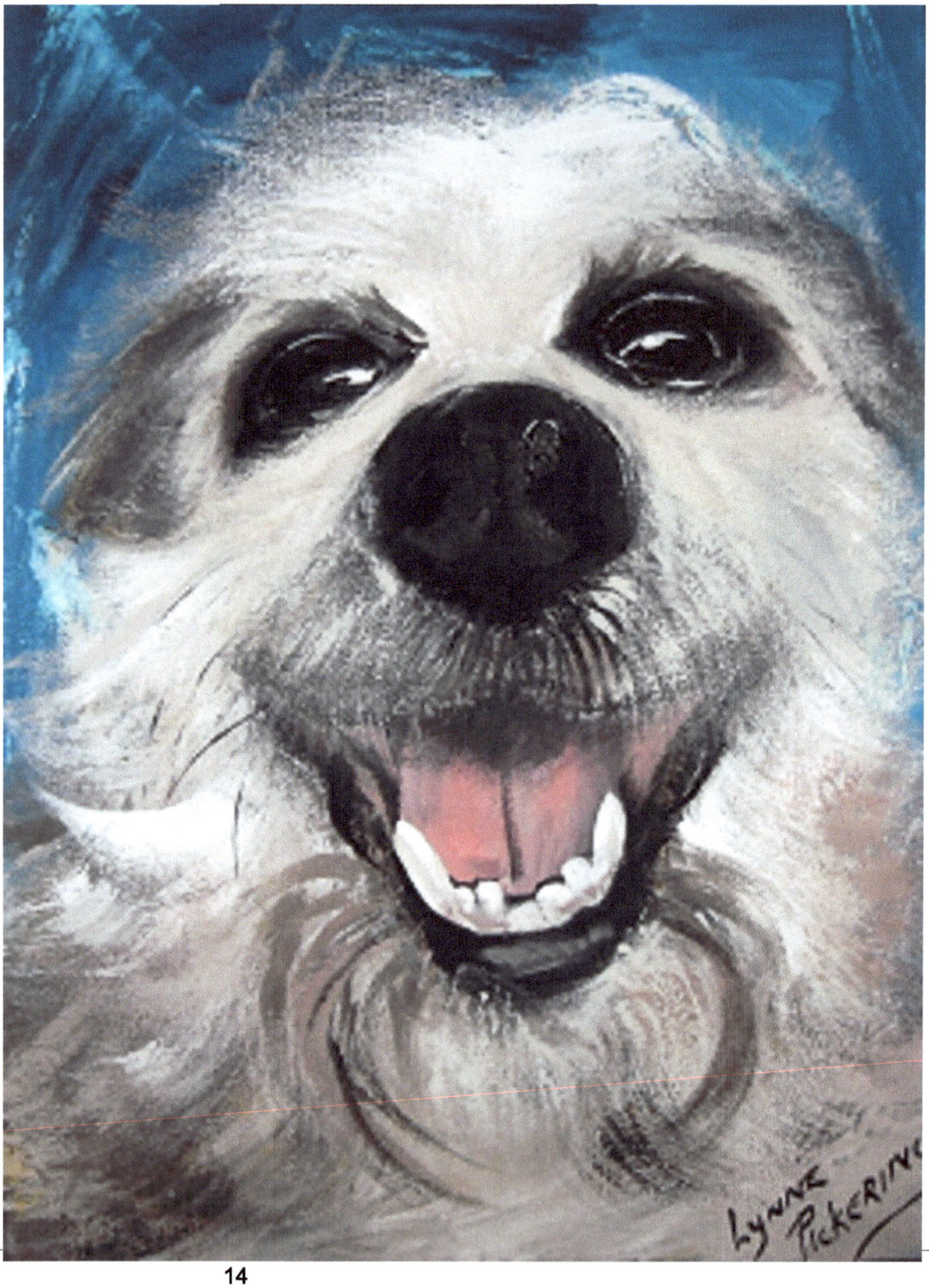
LYNNE

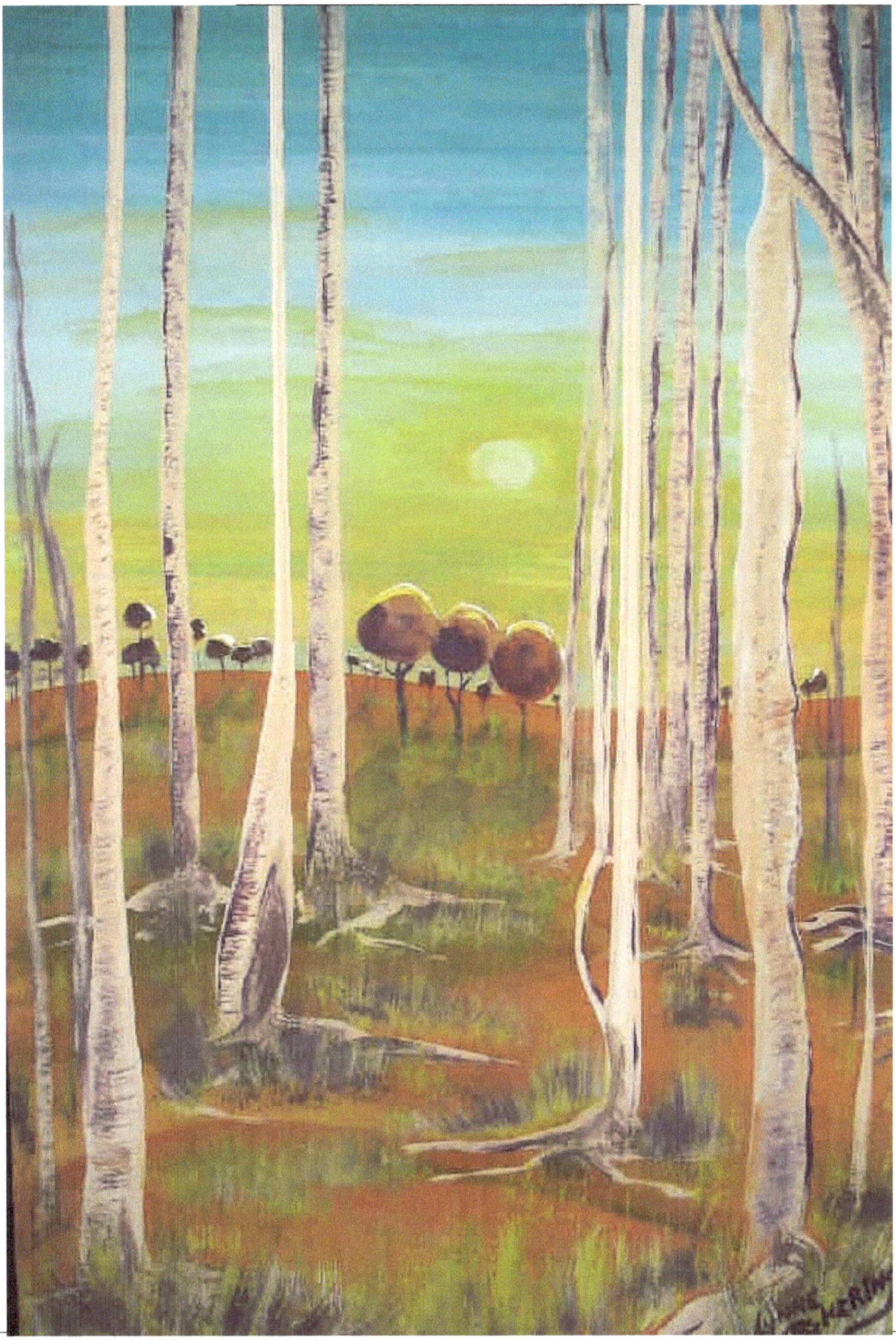

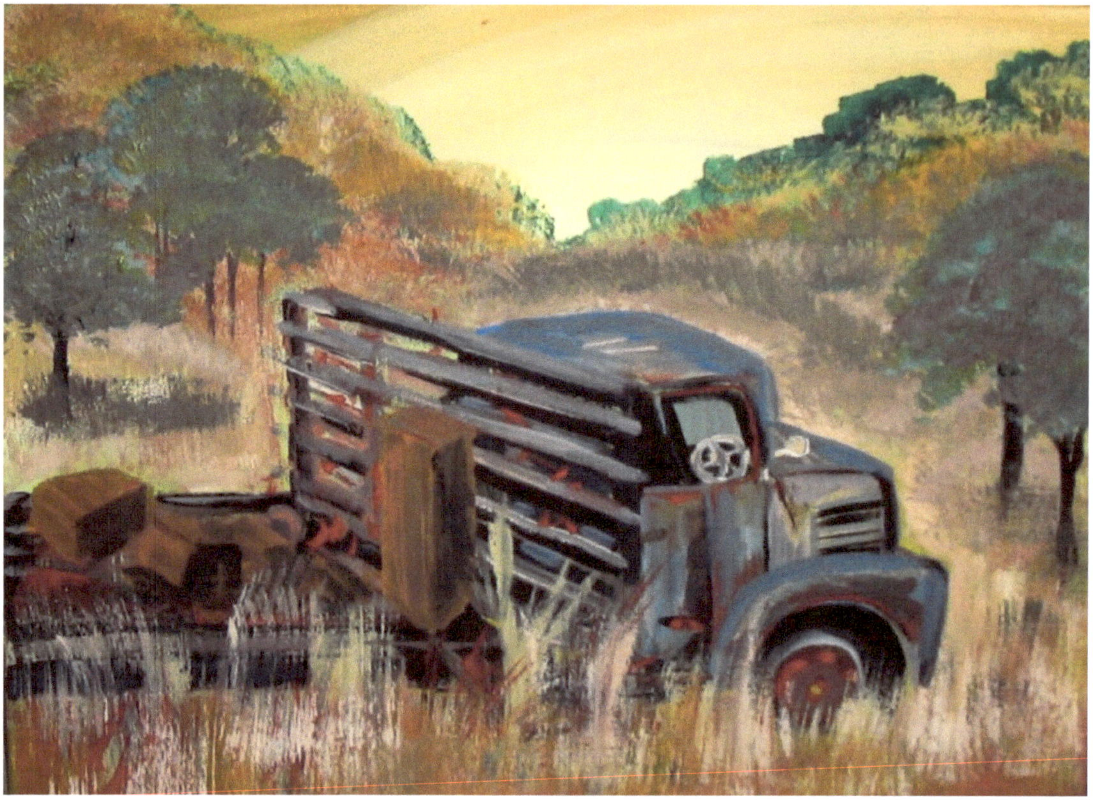

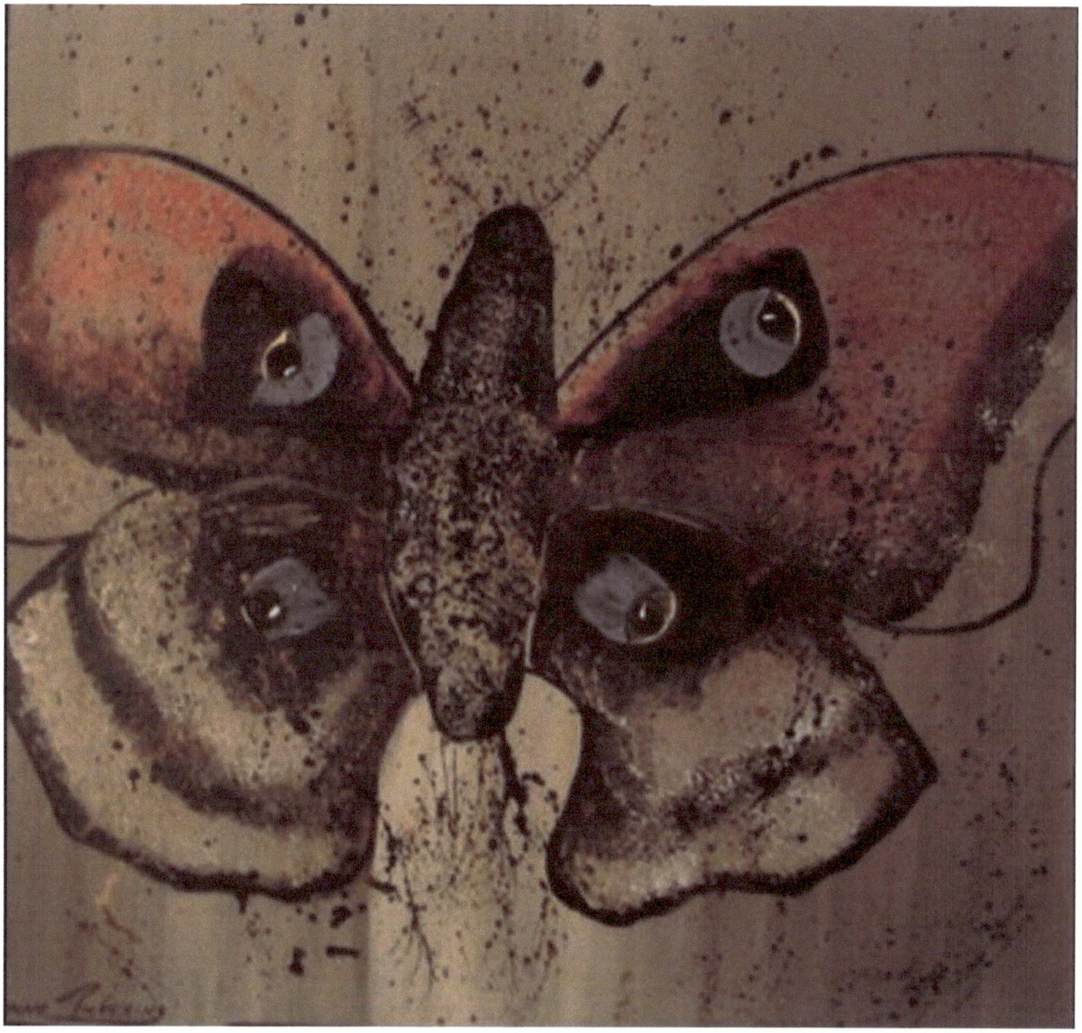

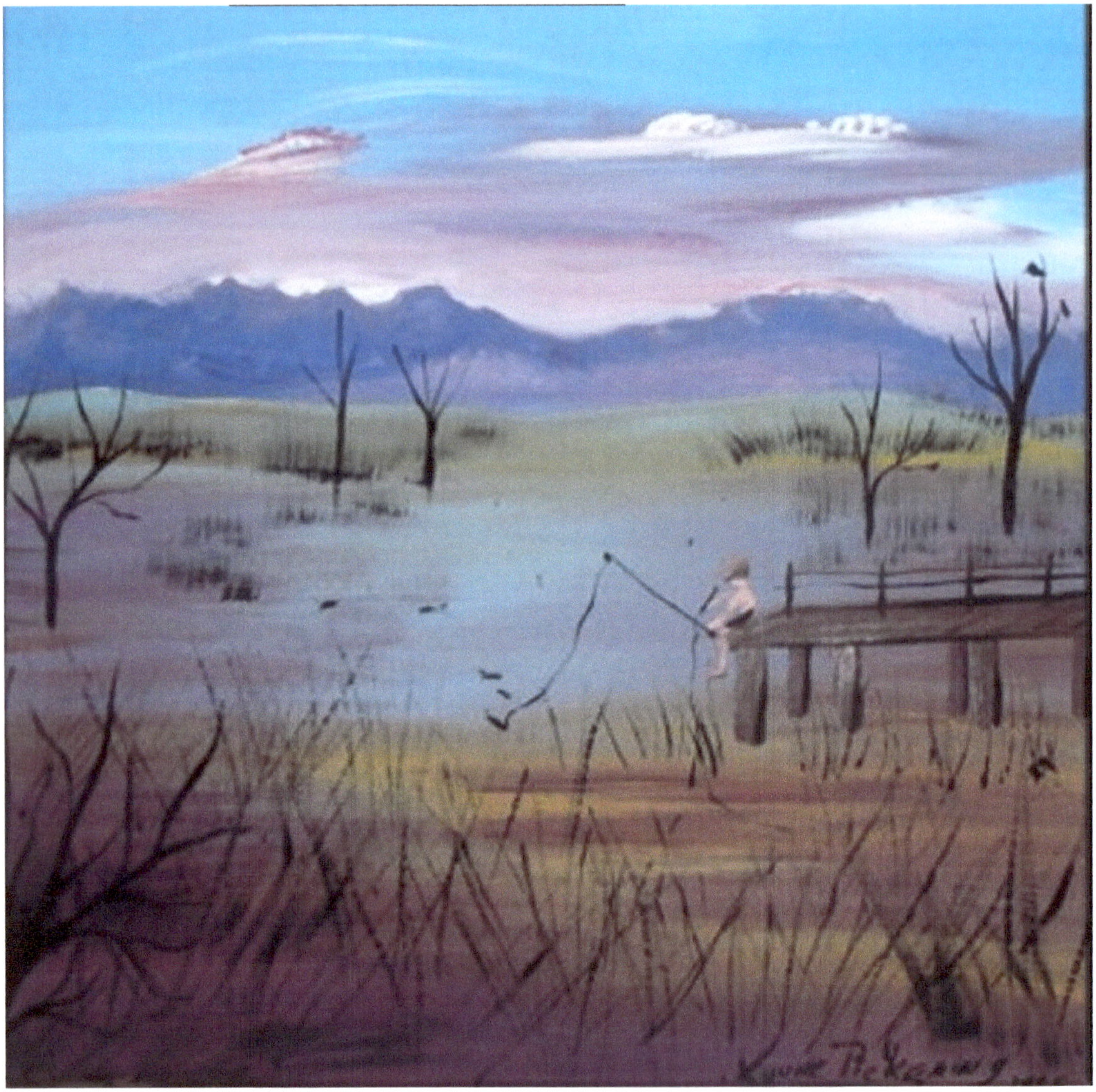

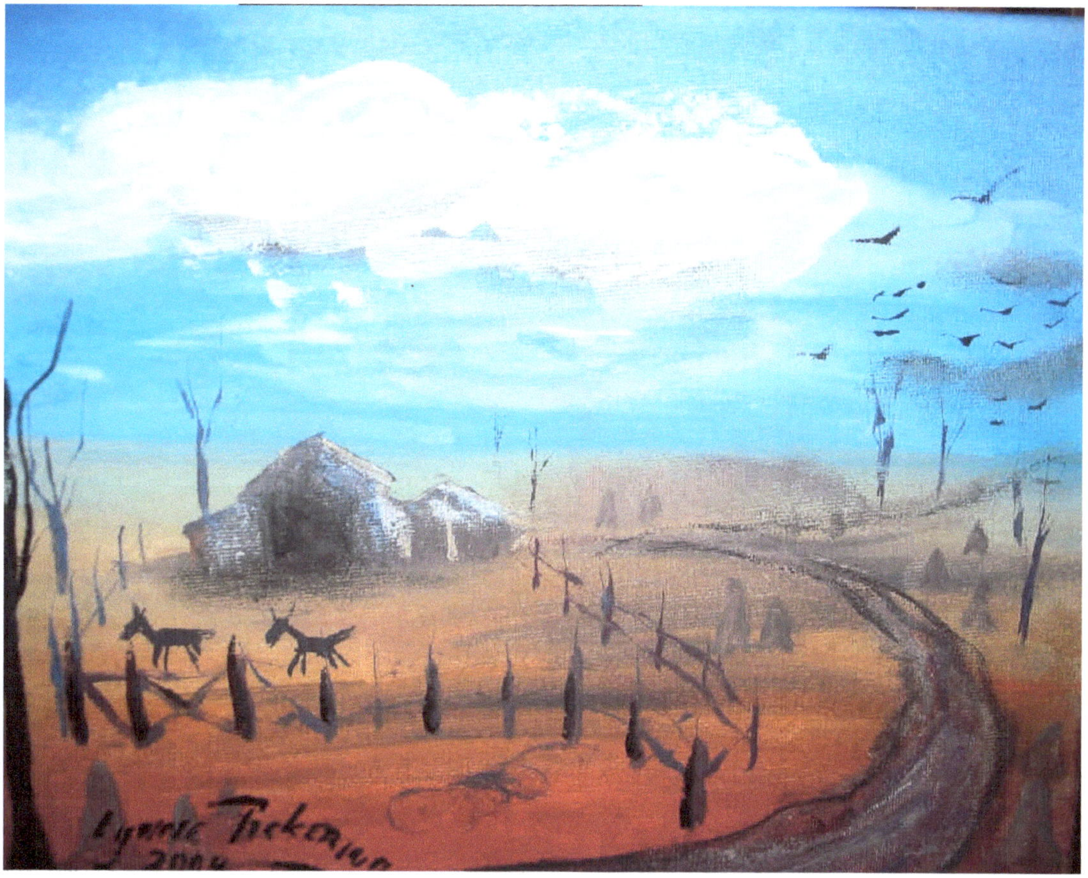
Lynne Pickering

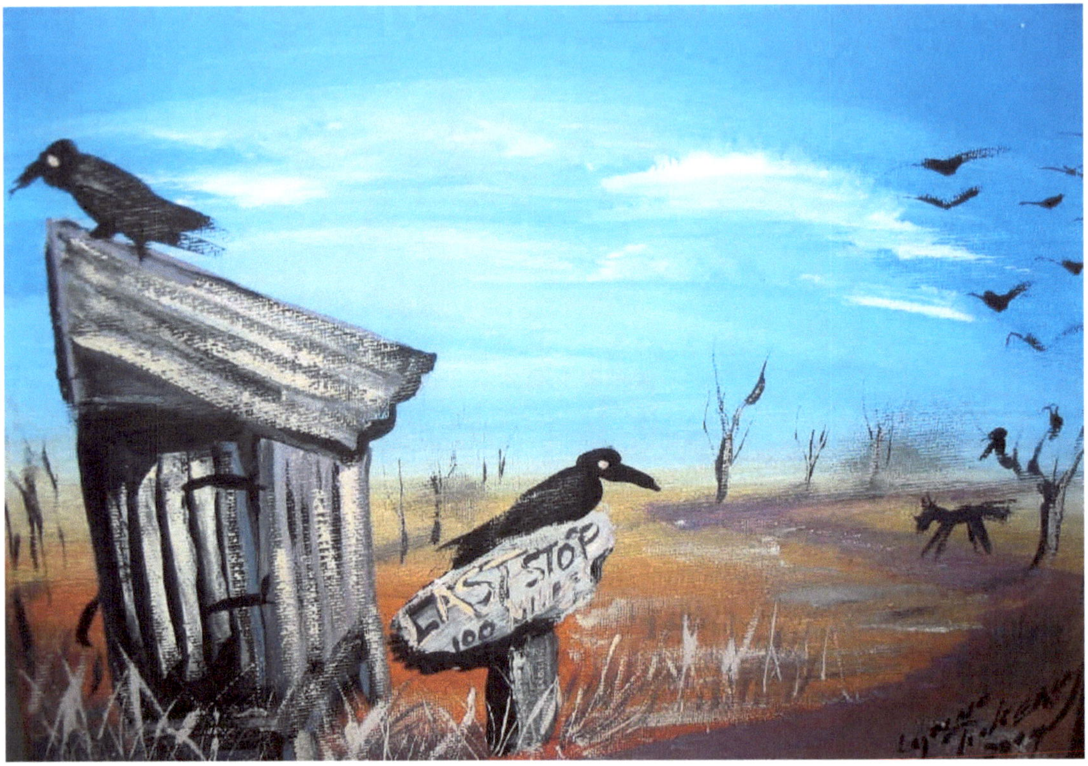
LAST STOP

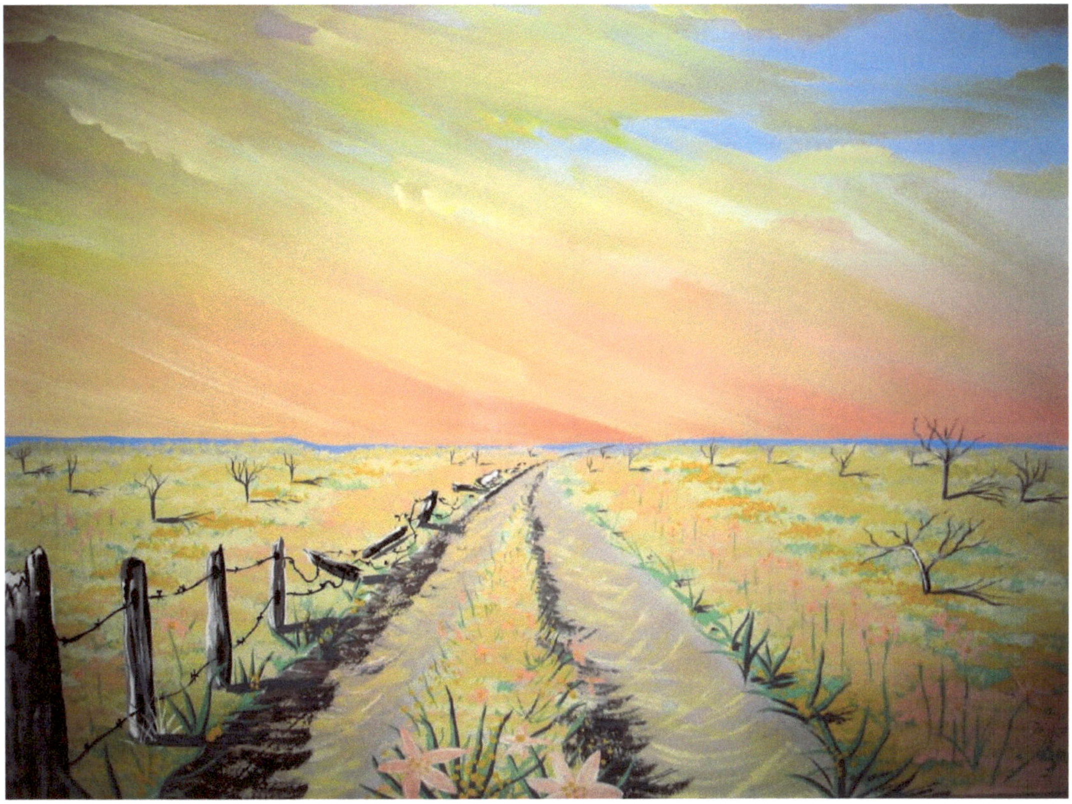

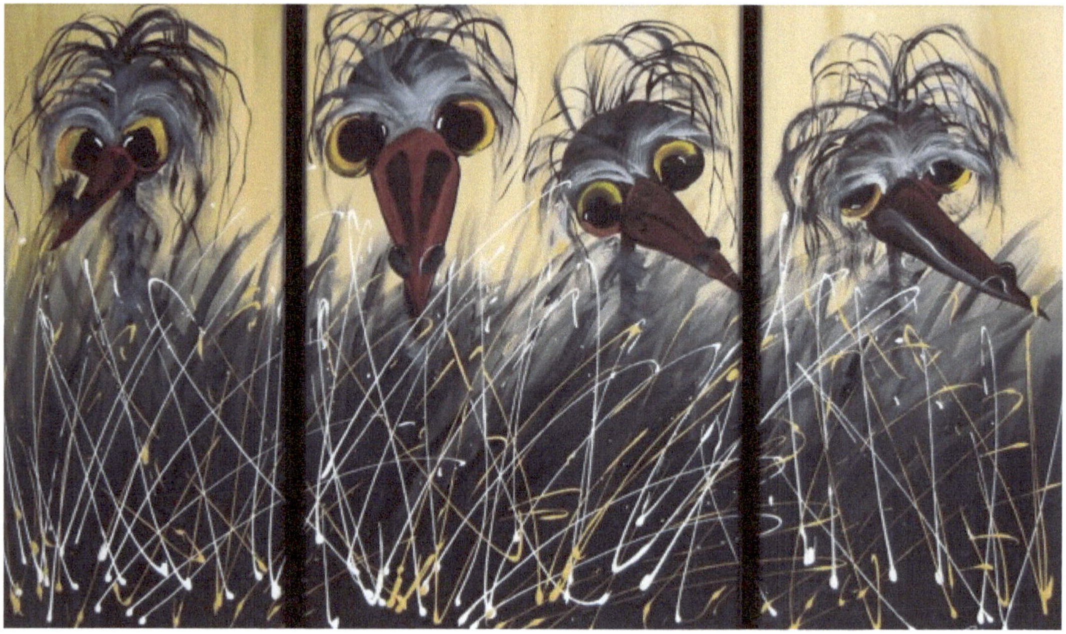

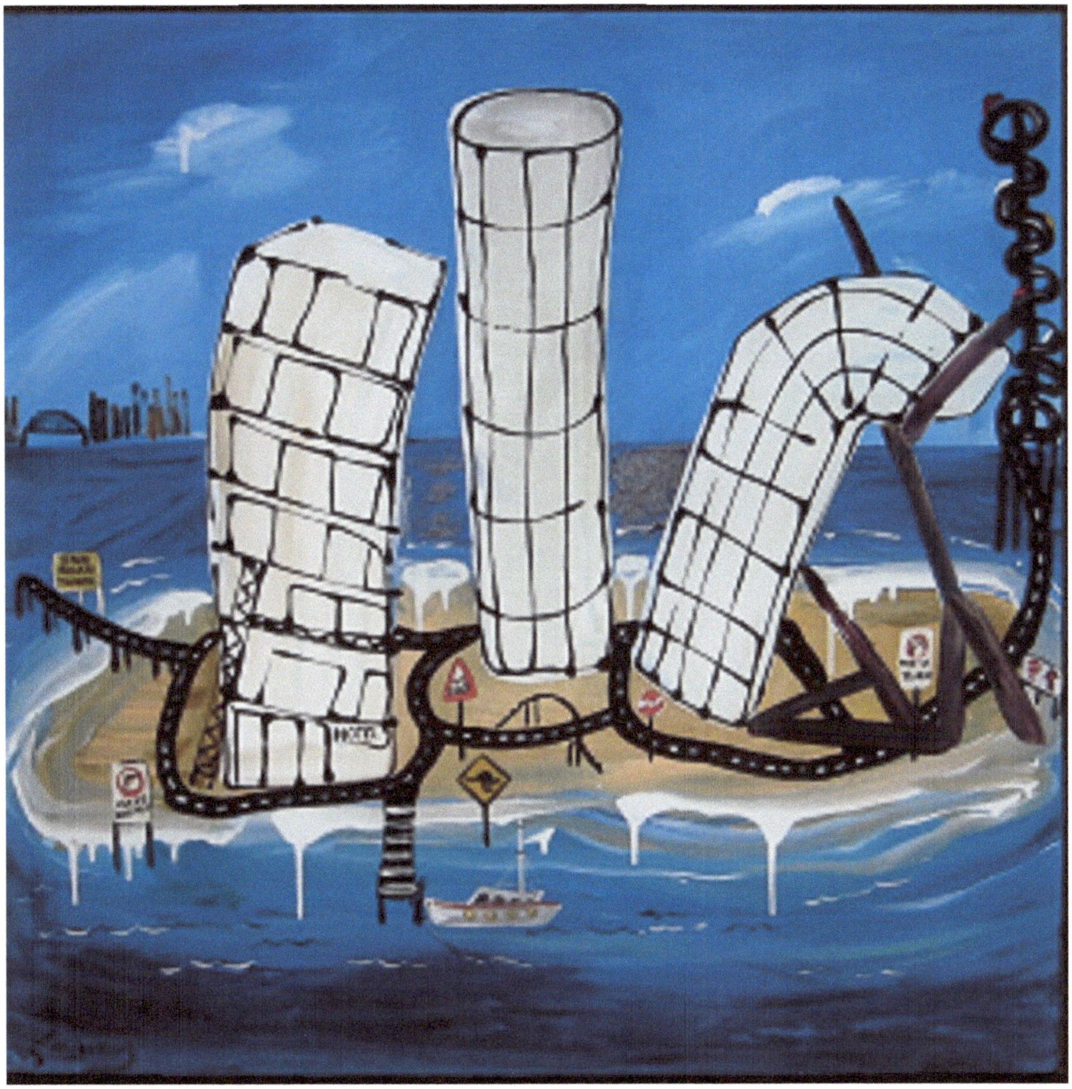

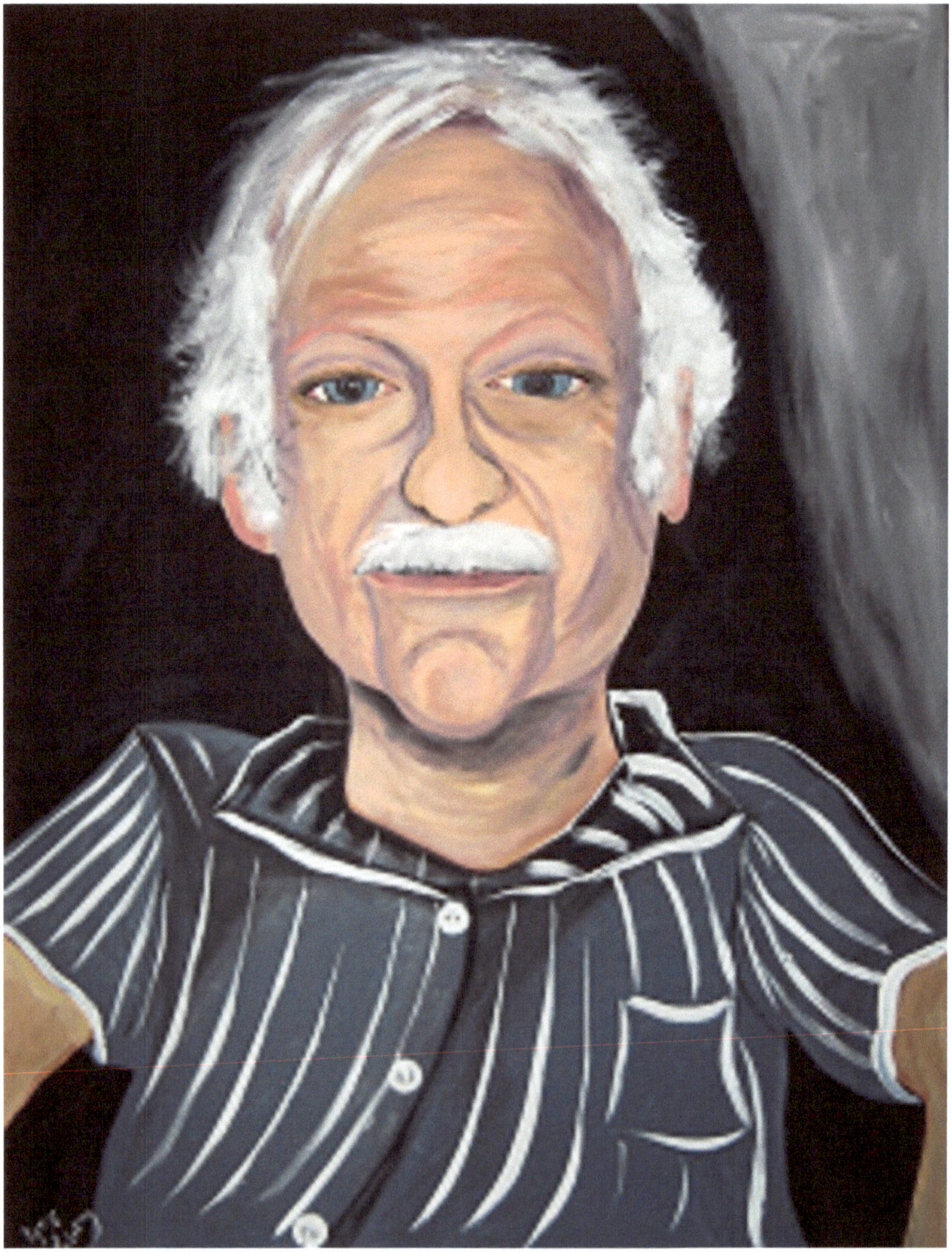

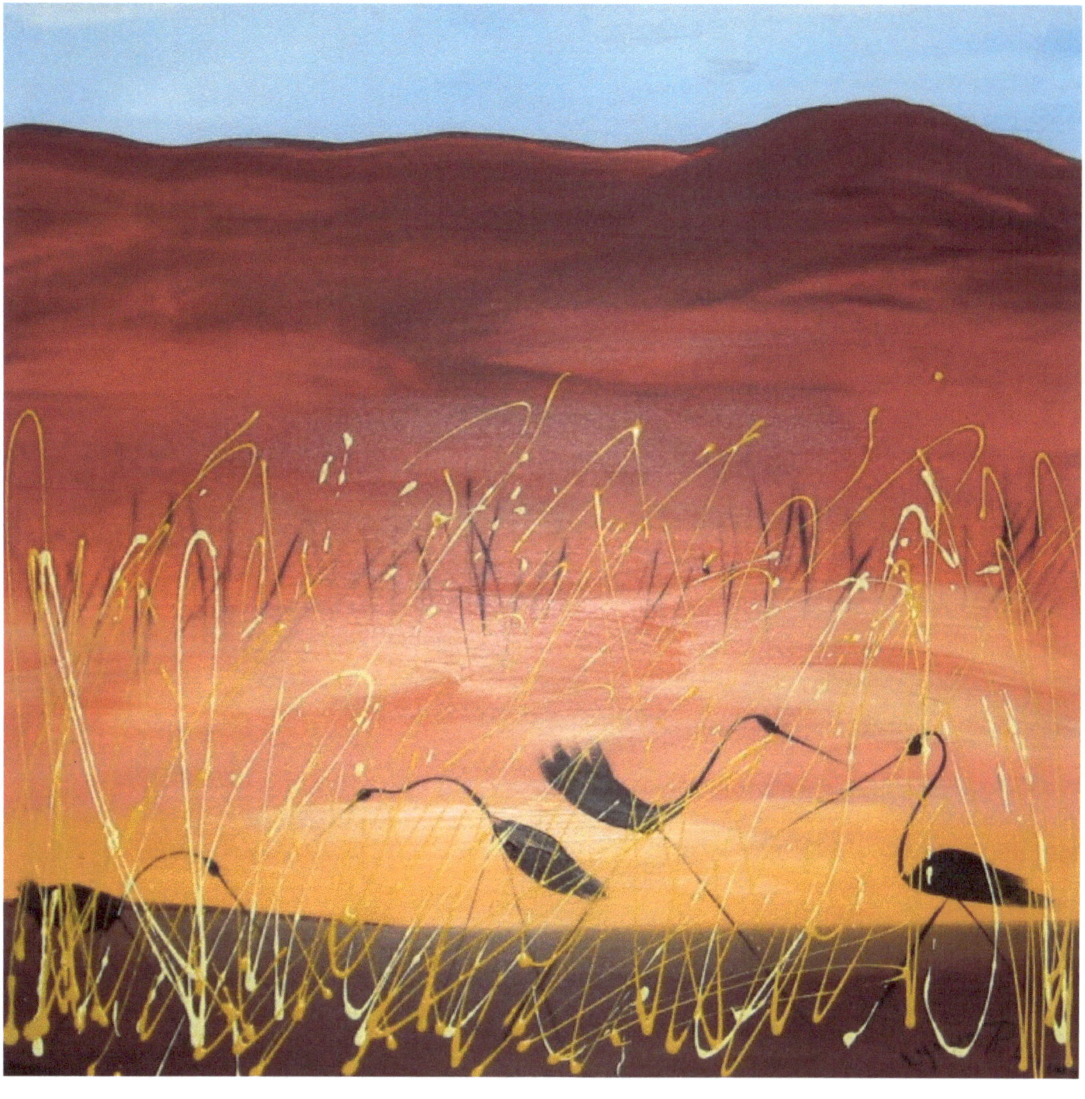

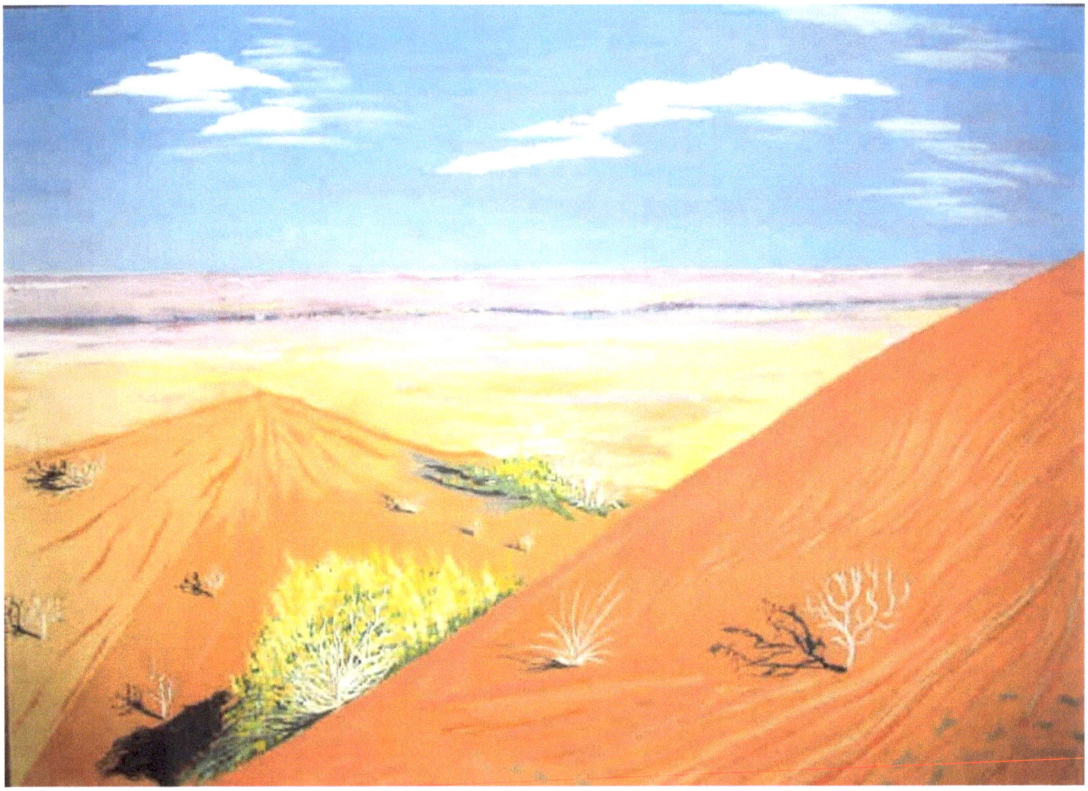

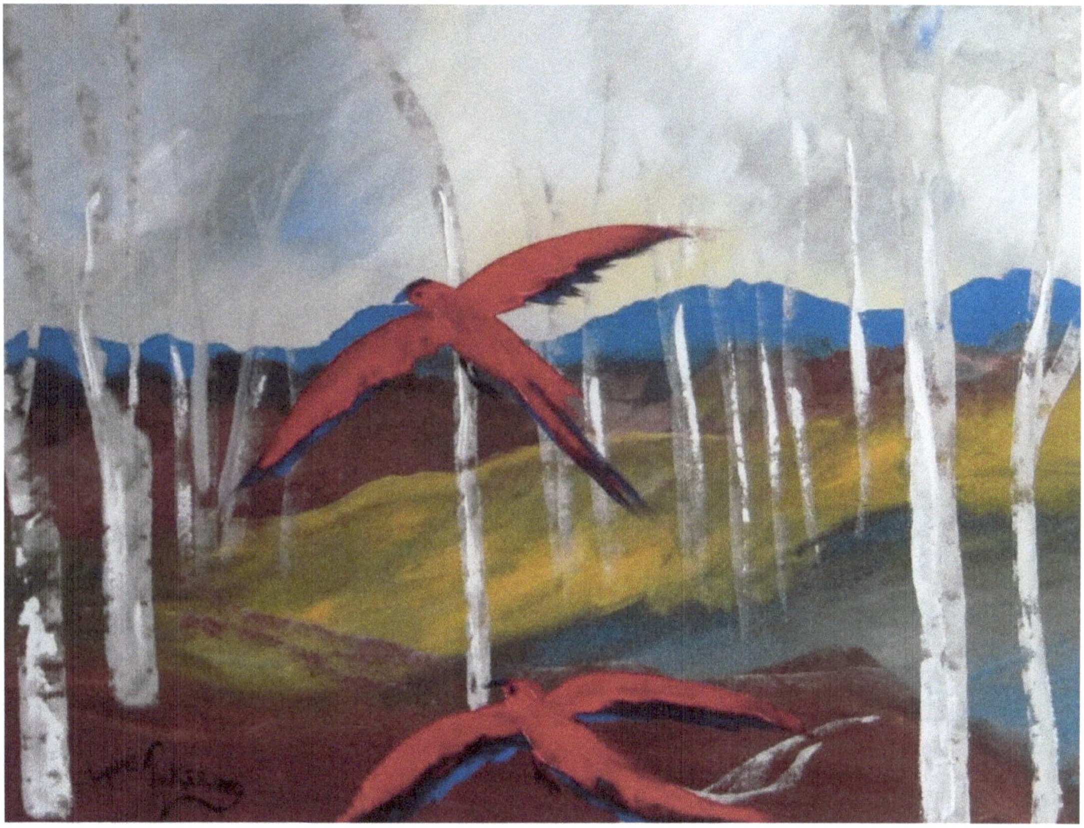

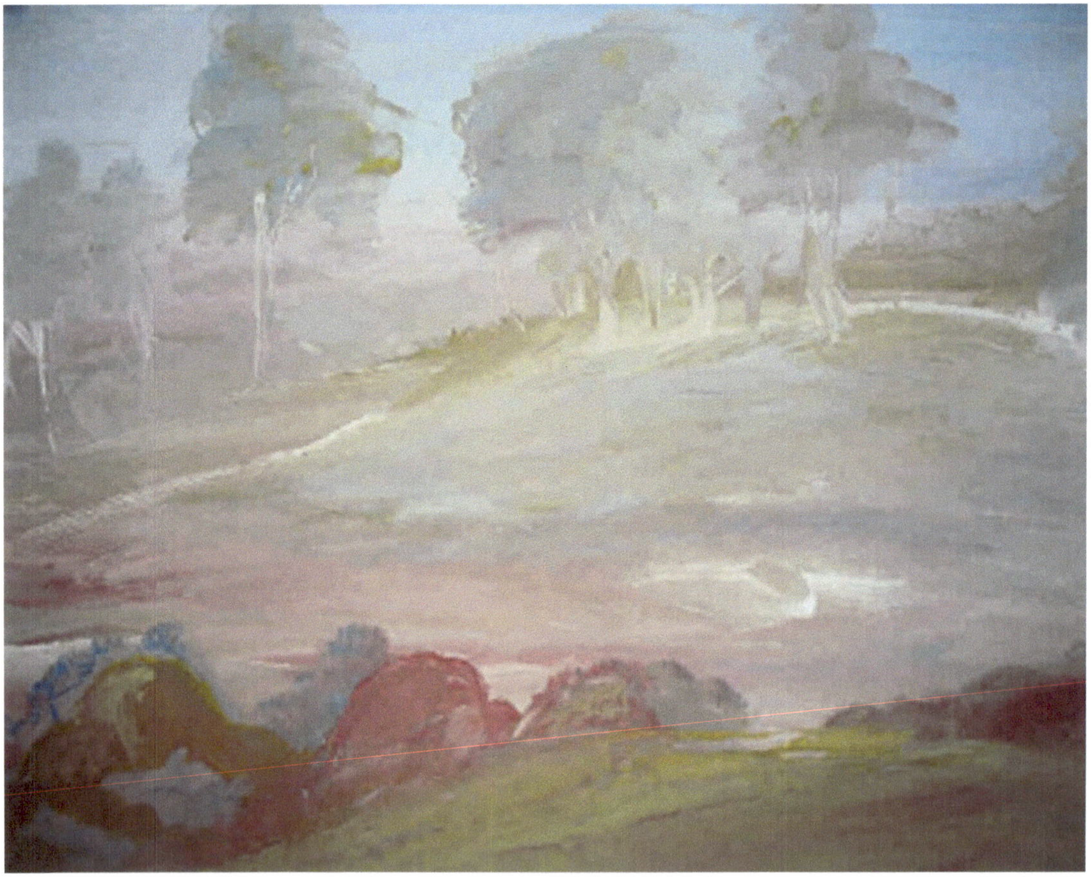

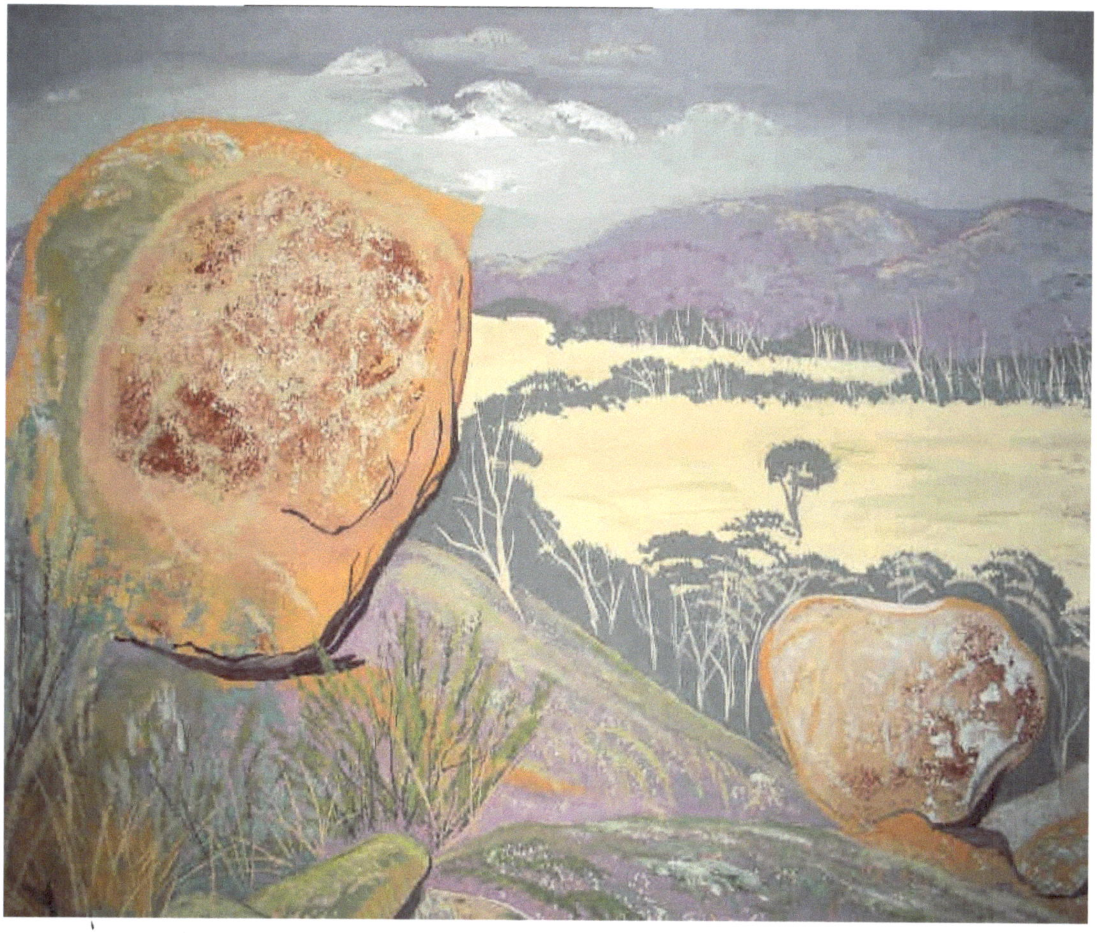

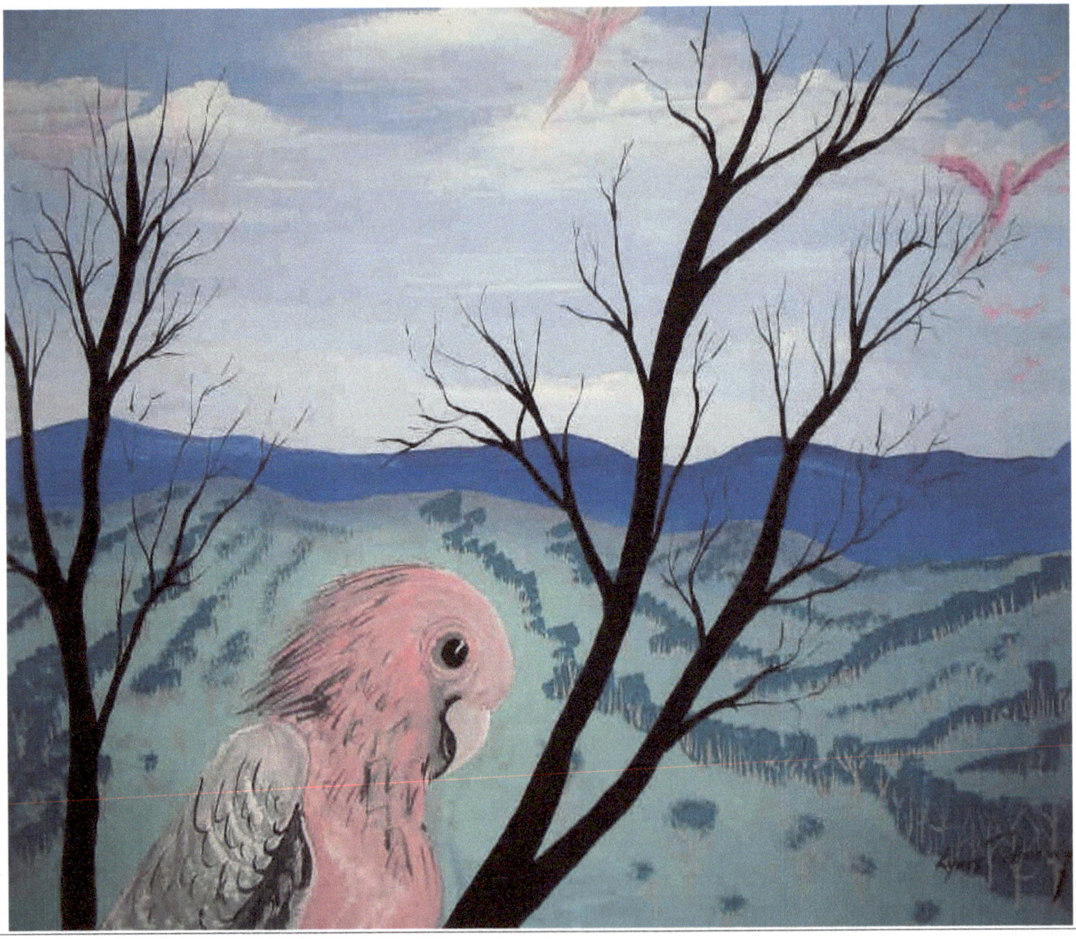

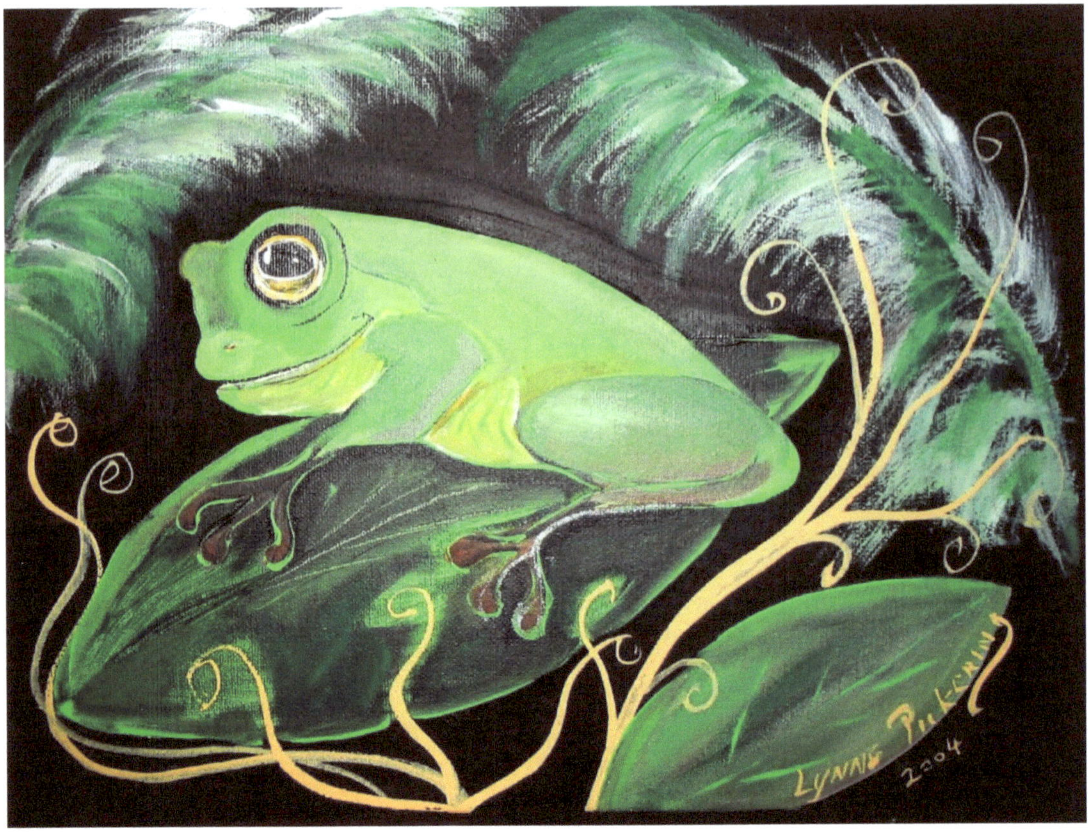
Lynne Pickering
2004

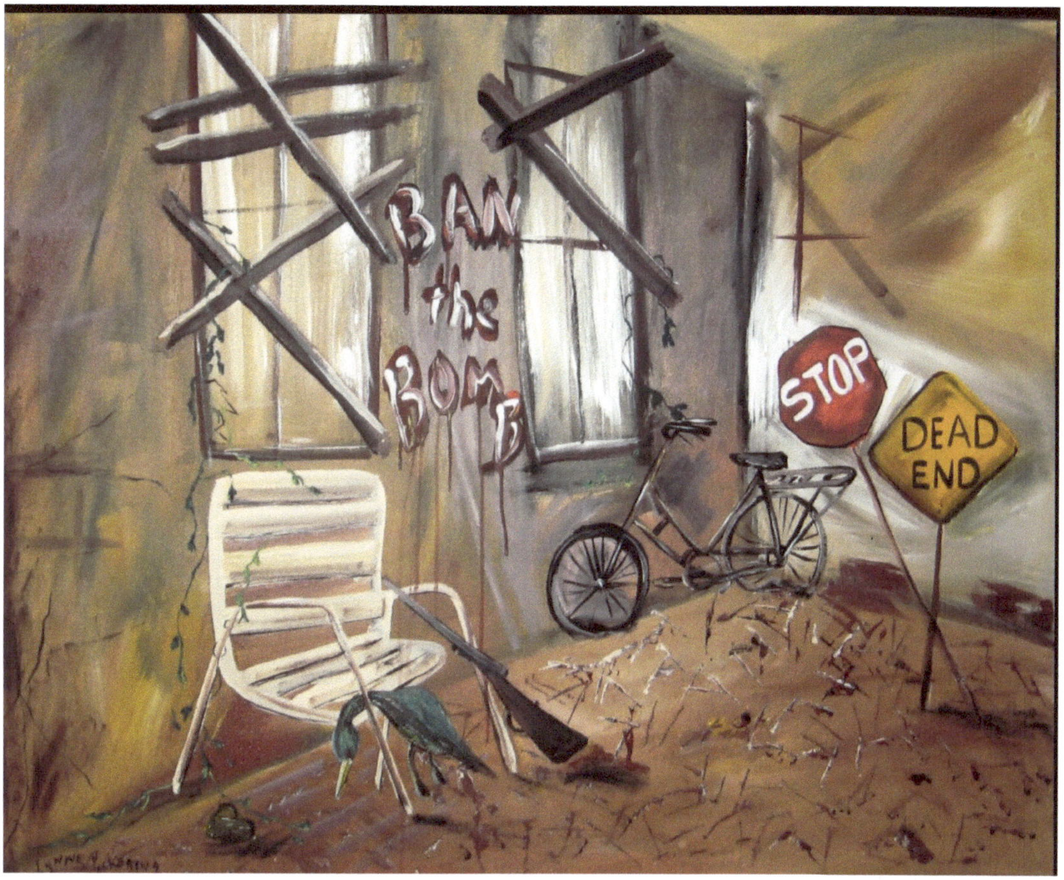
BAN
the
BOMB
STOP
DEAD
END

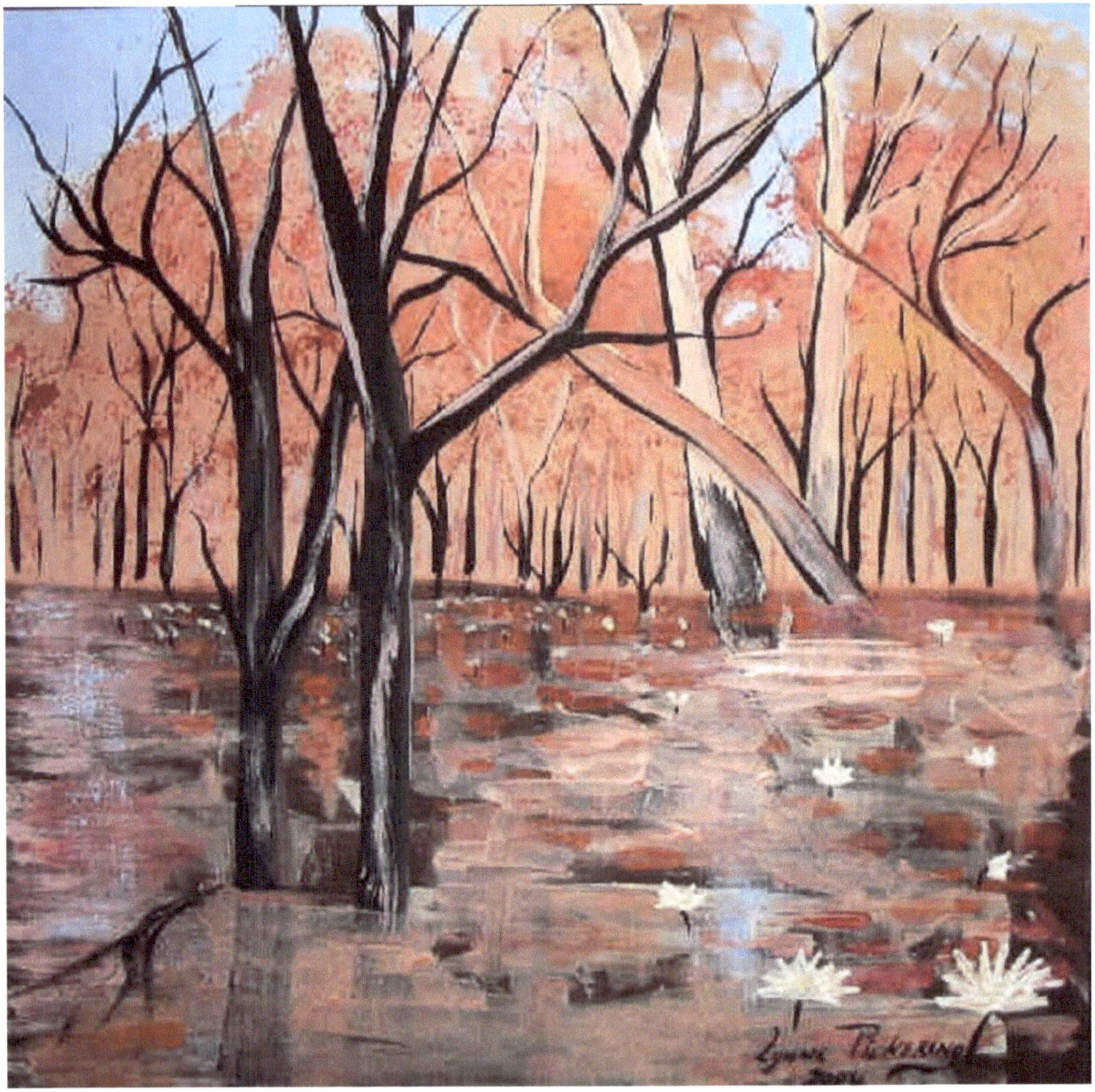
Lynne Pickering

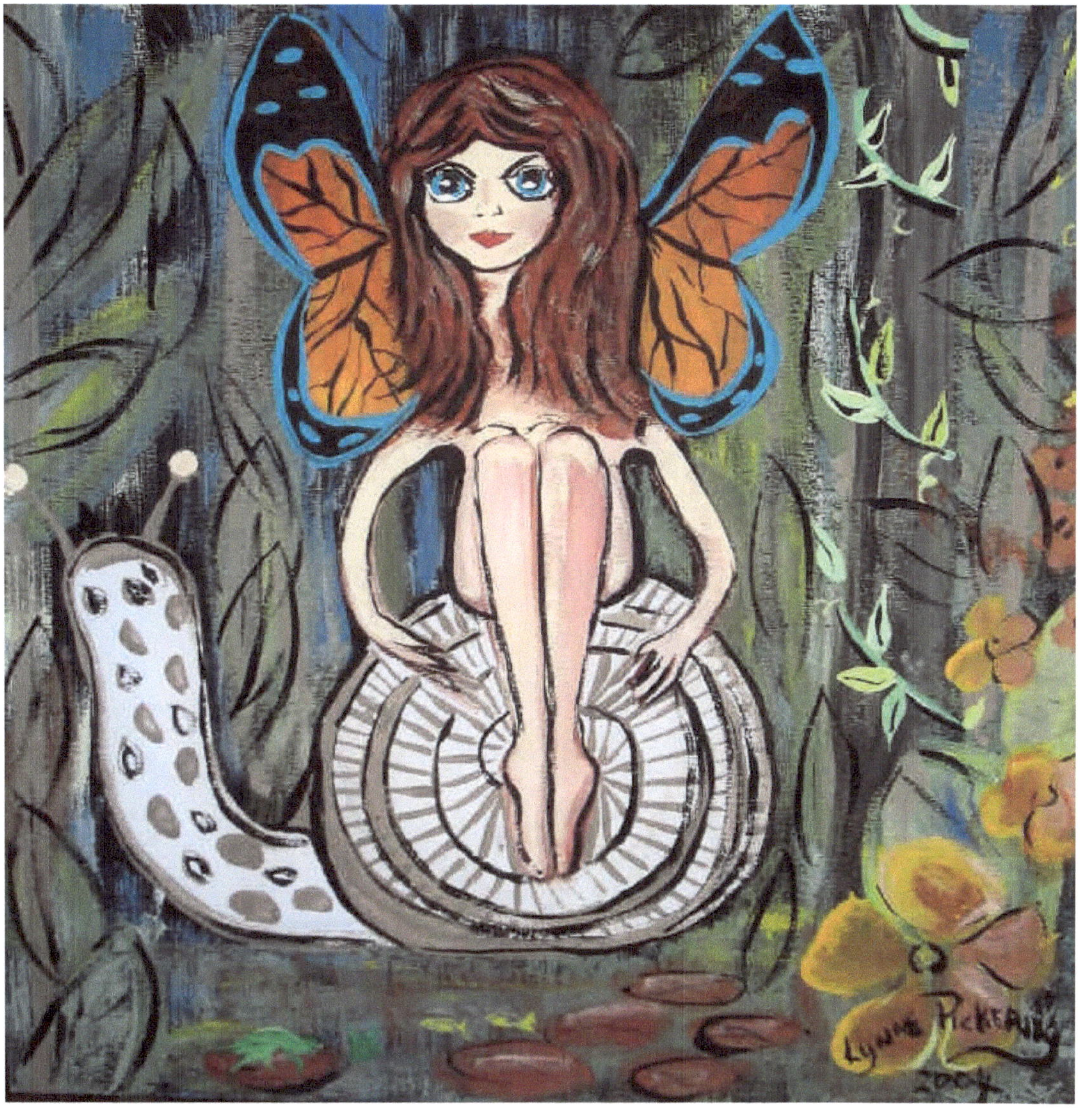
Lynne Pickering
2004

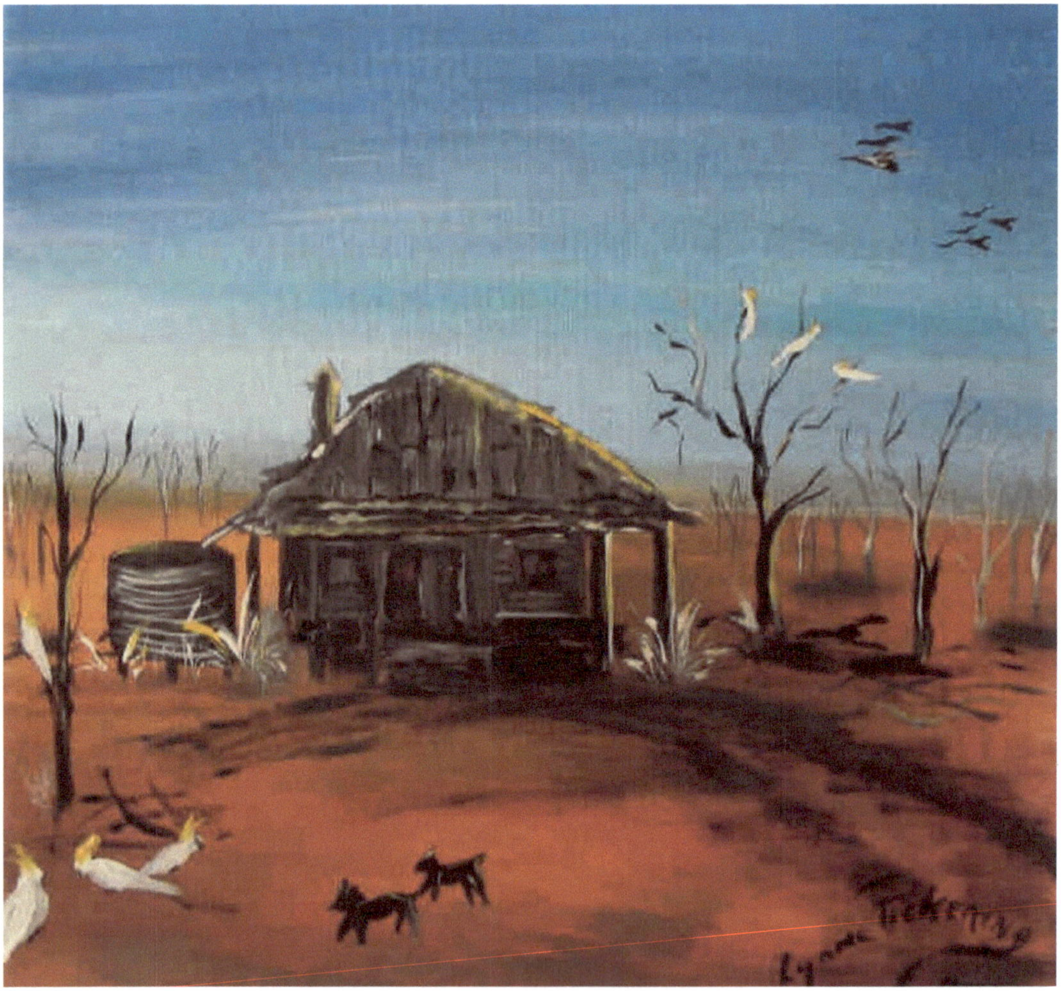
Lynne Pickering

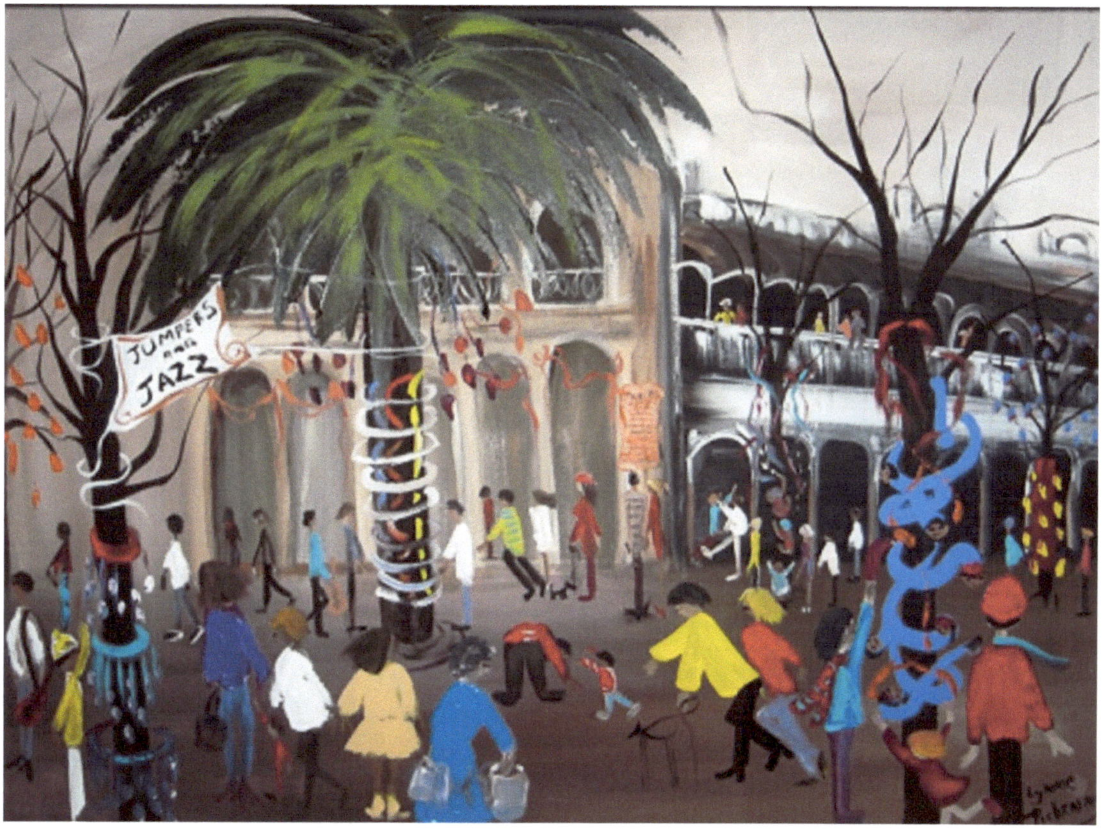
JUMPERS
and
JAZZ

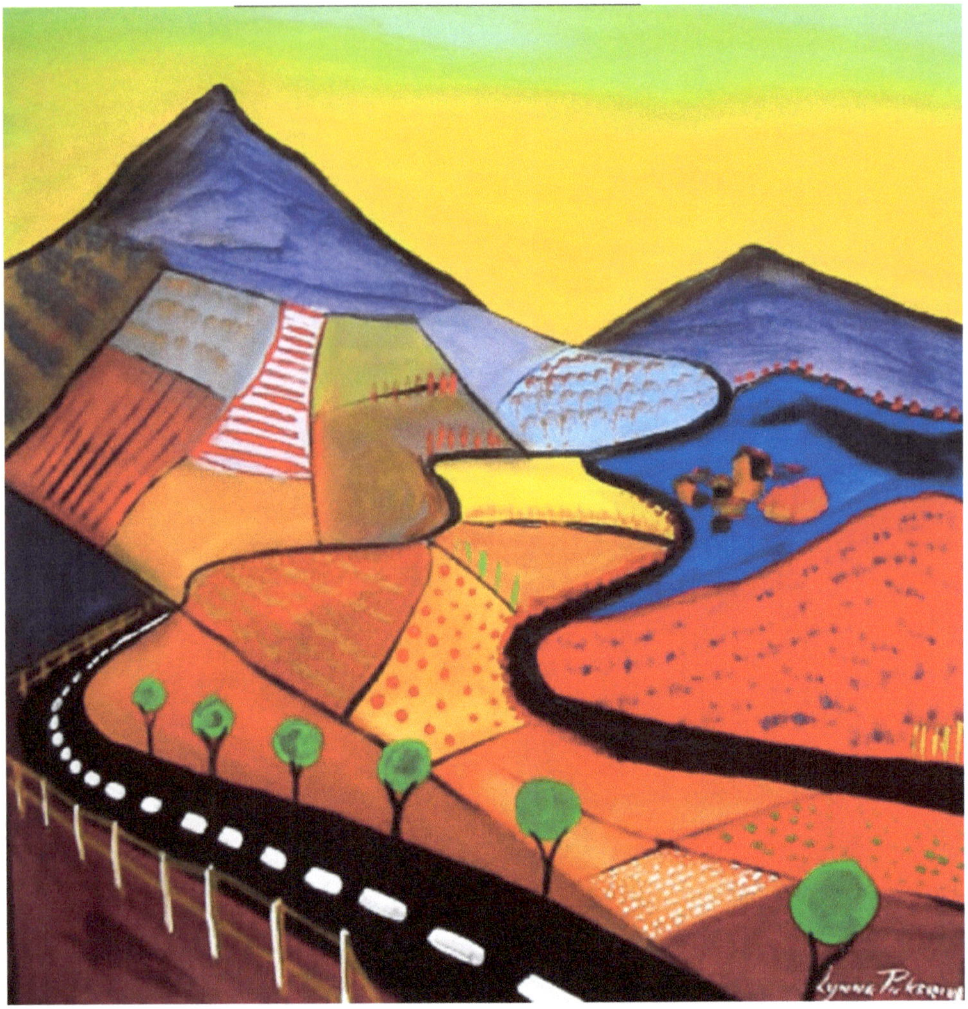
Lynne Pickering

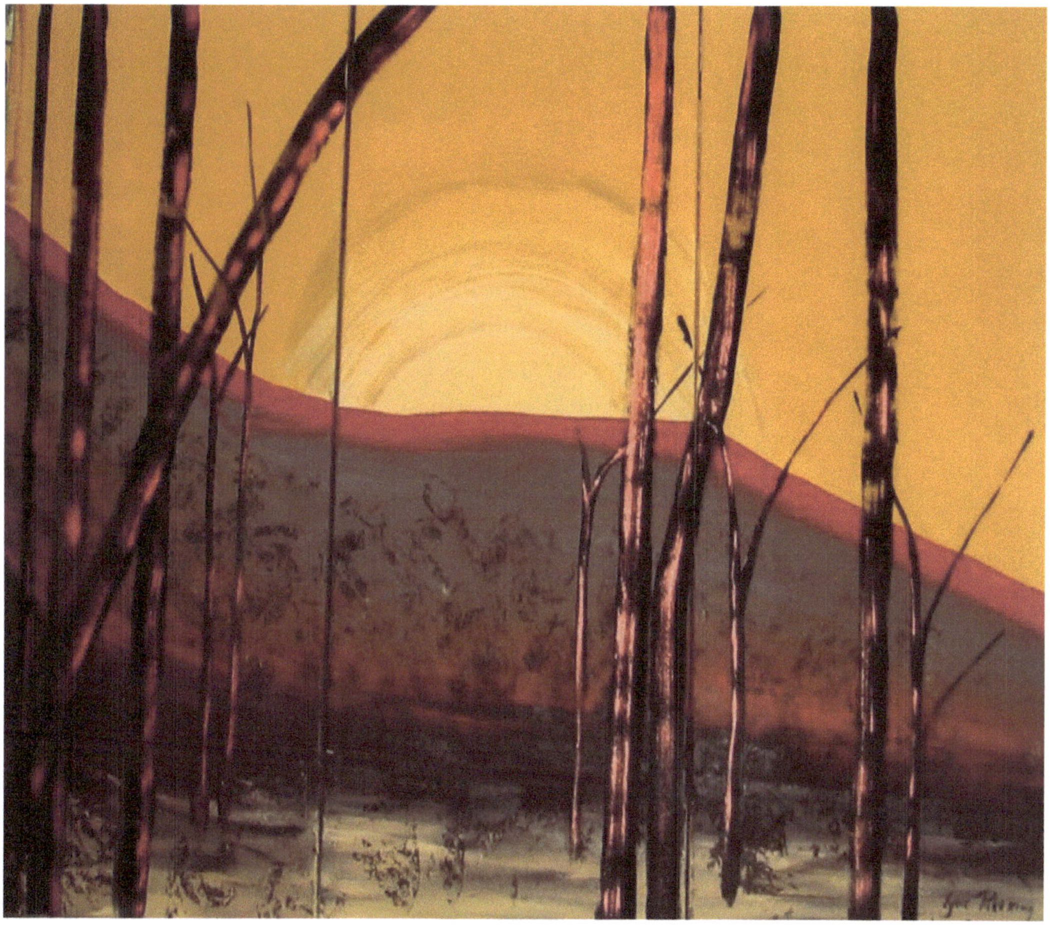

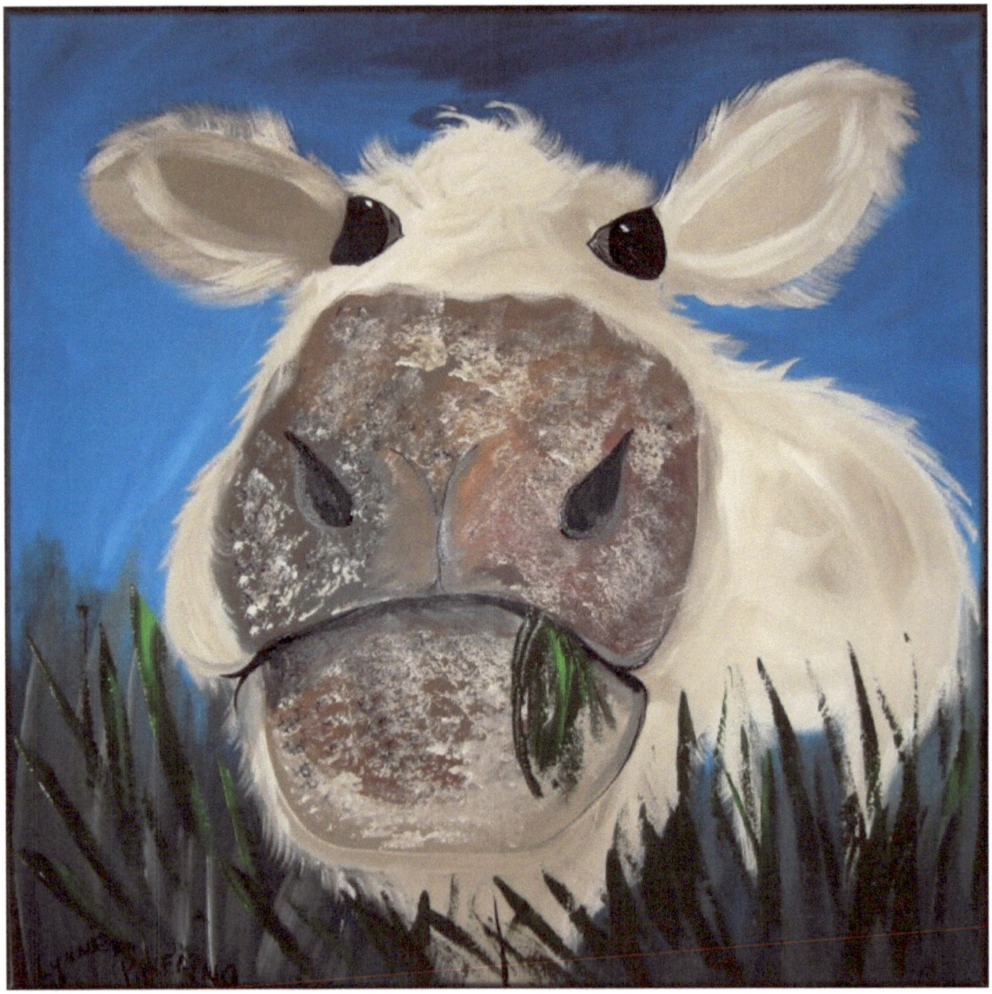

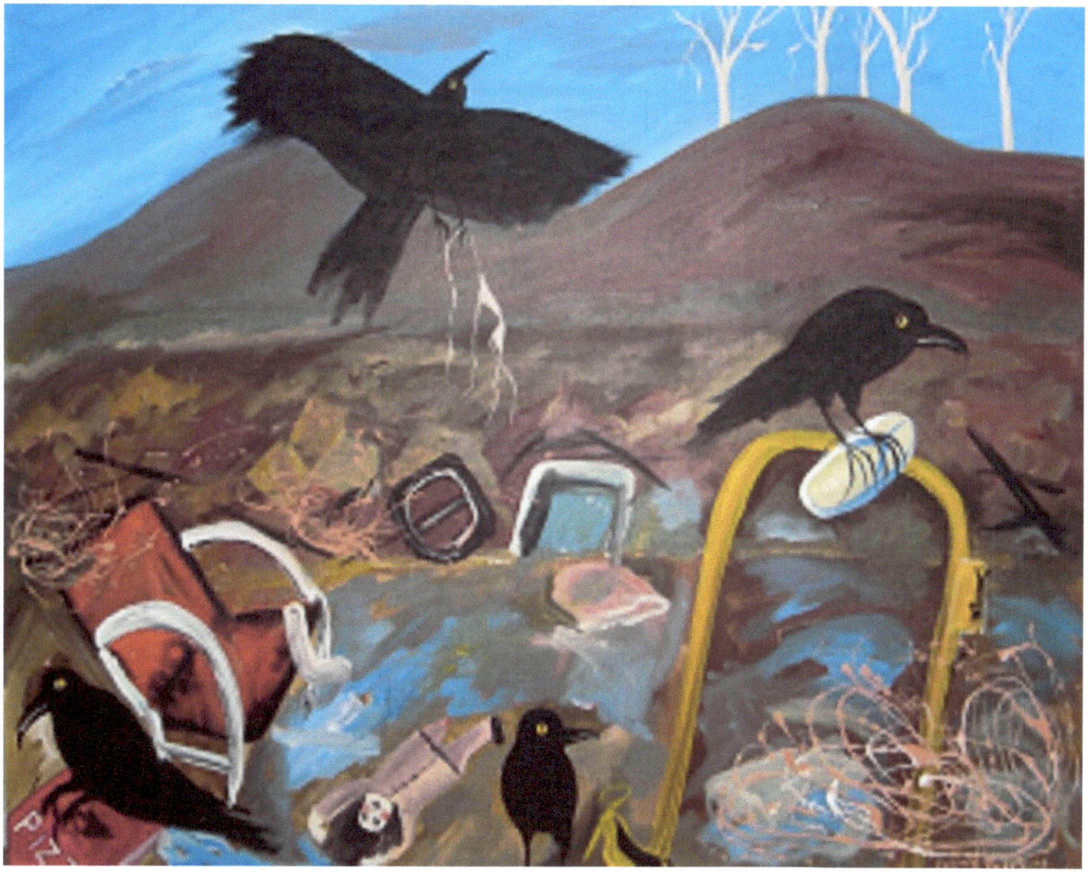

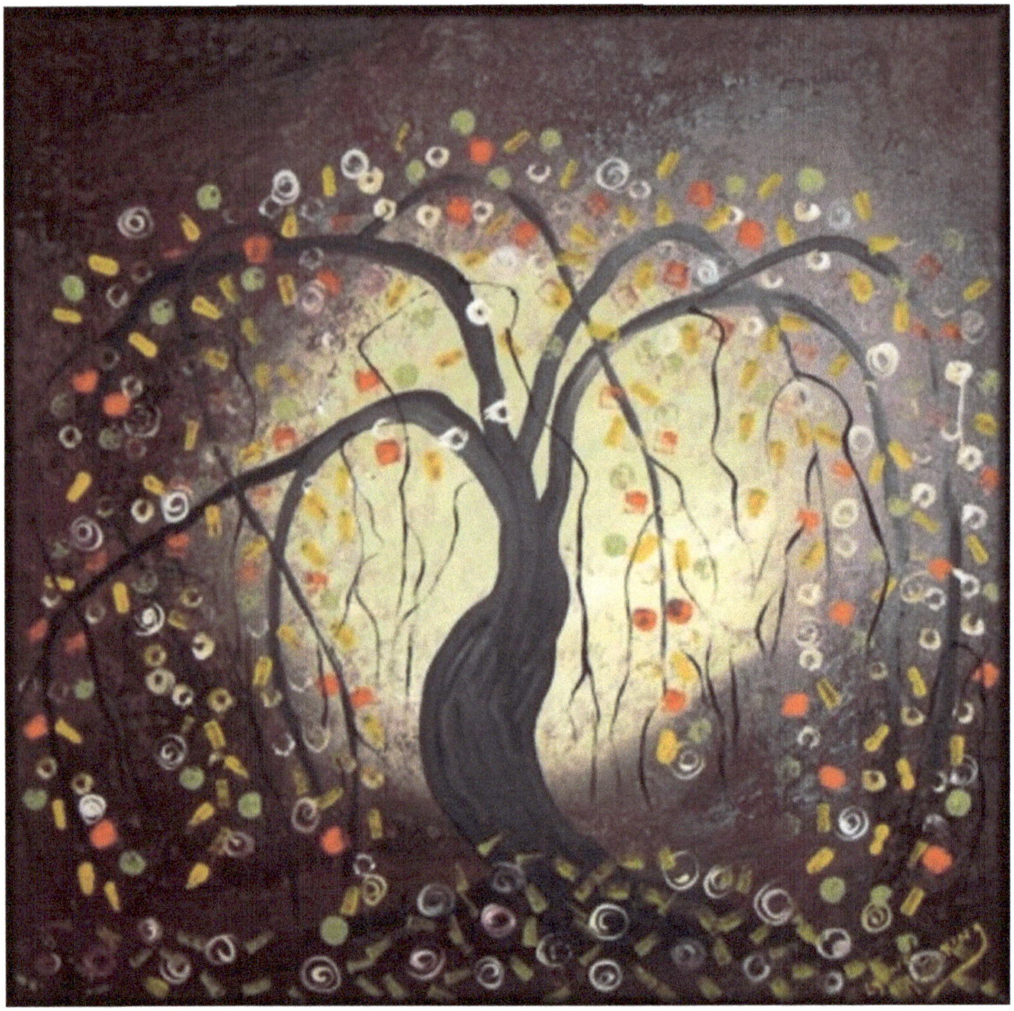

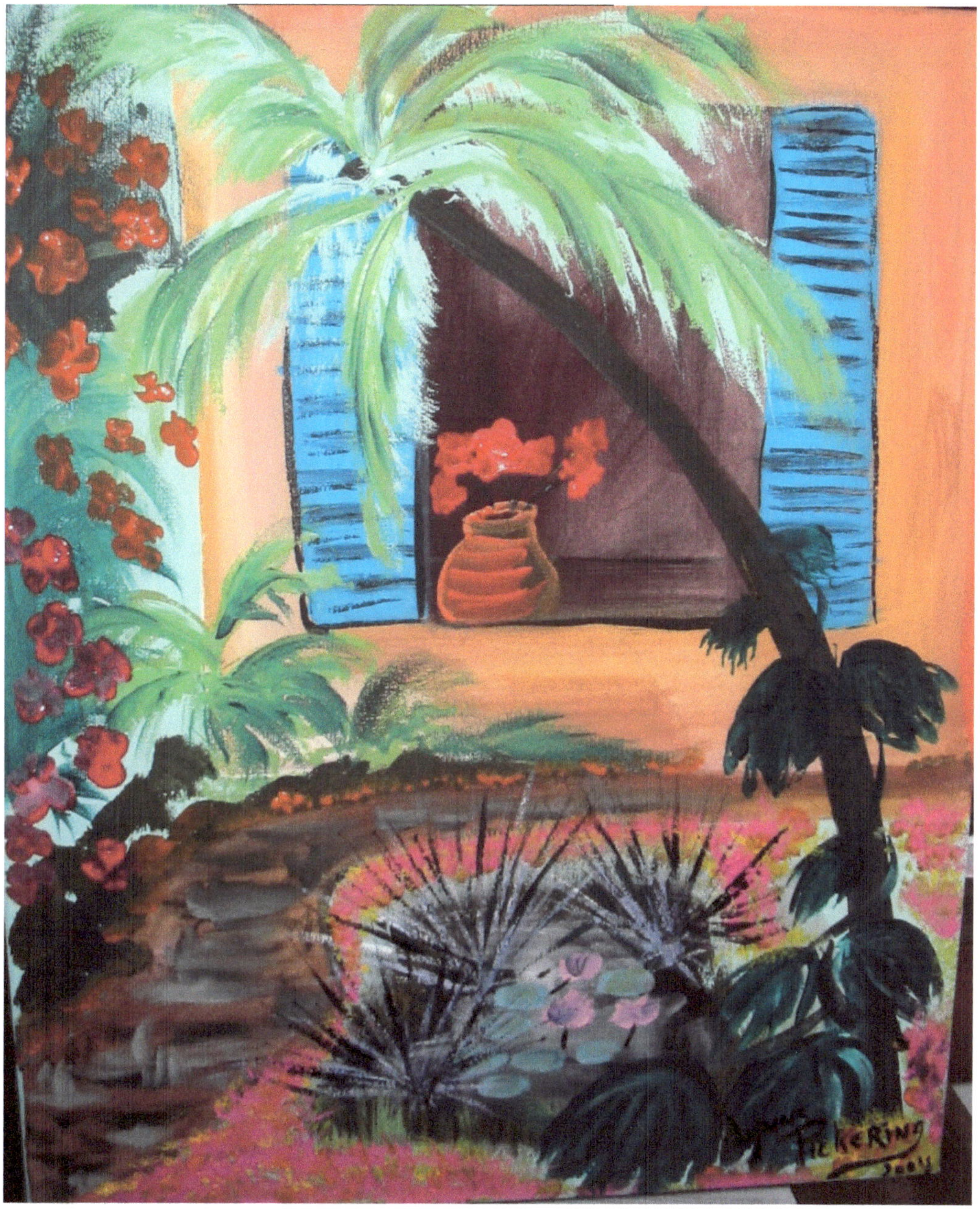
PICKERING

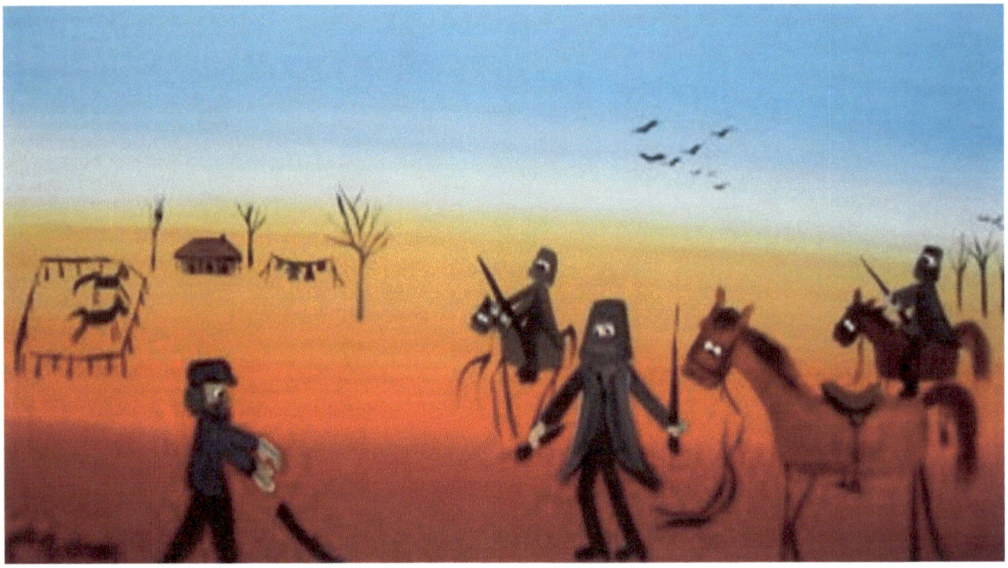

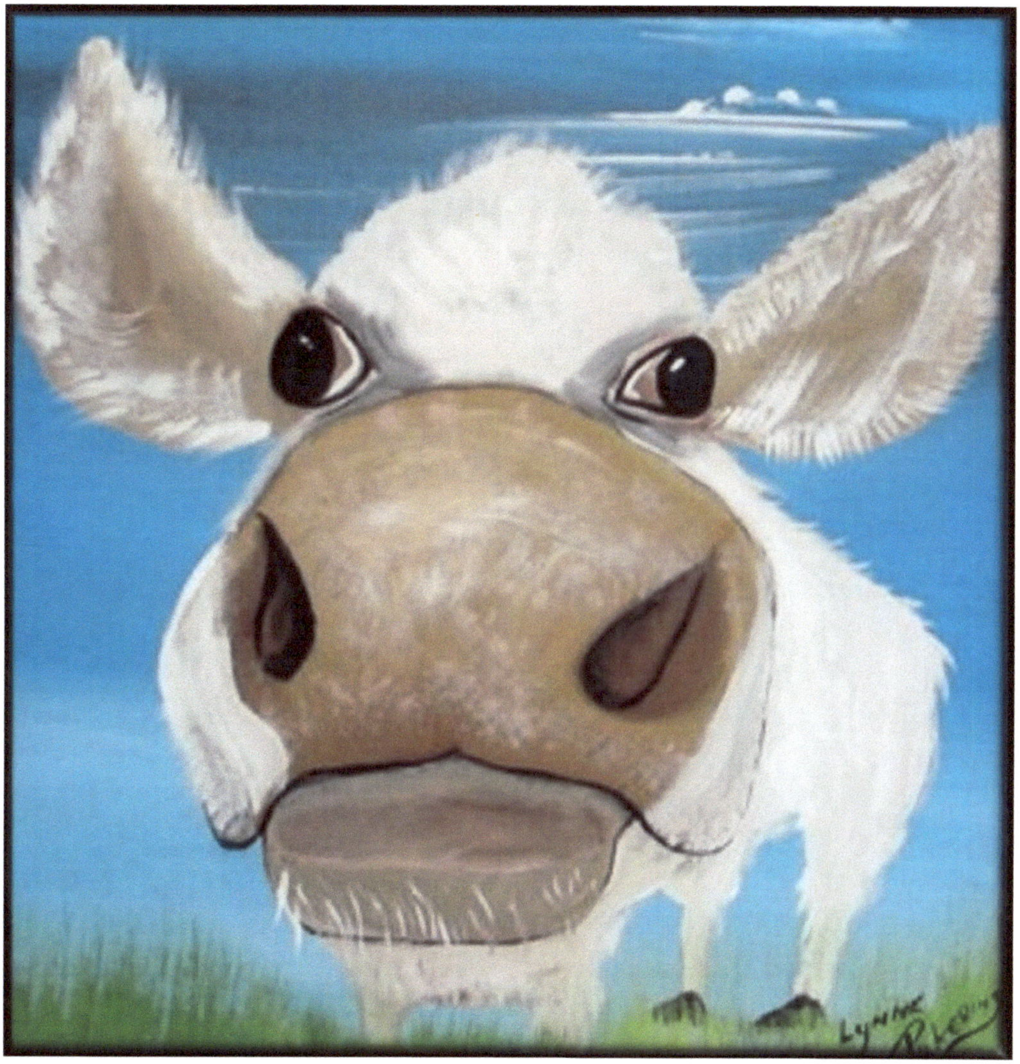

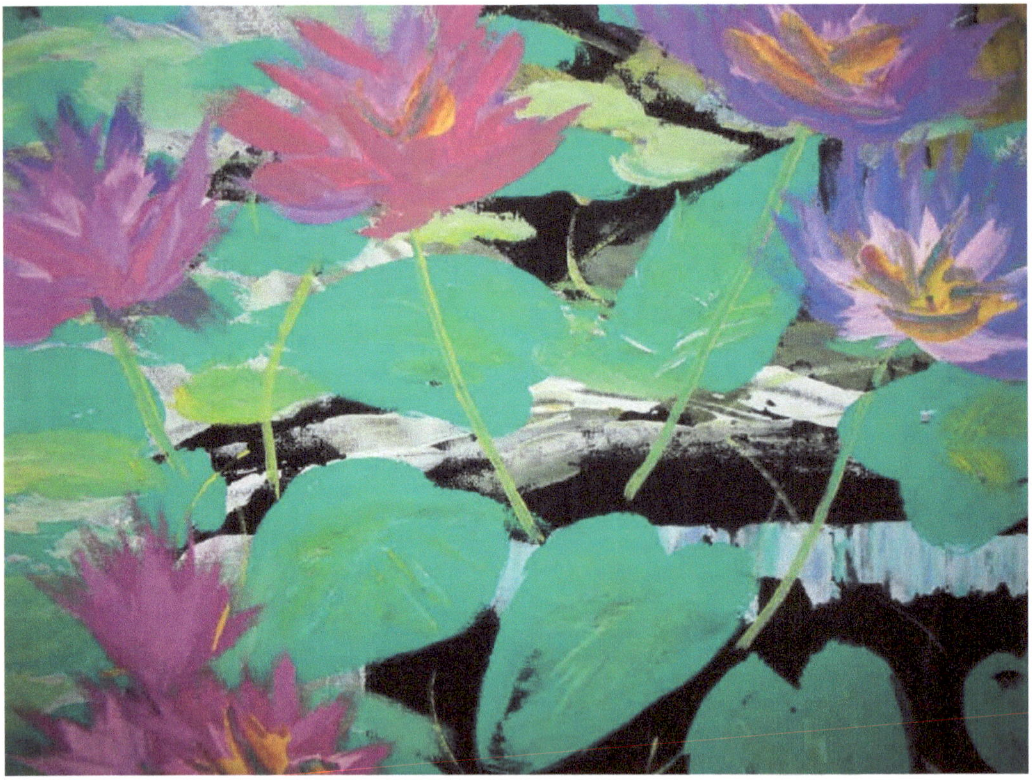

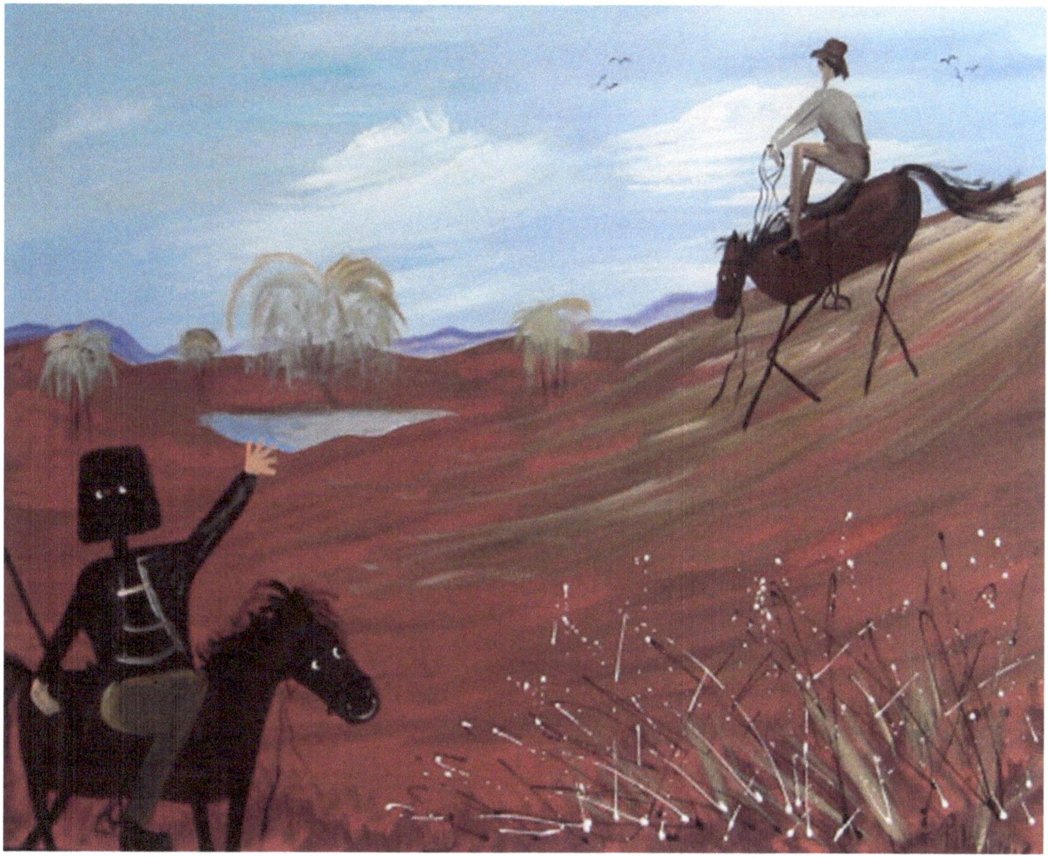

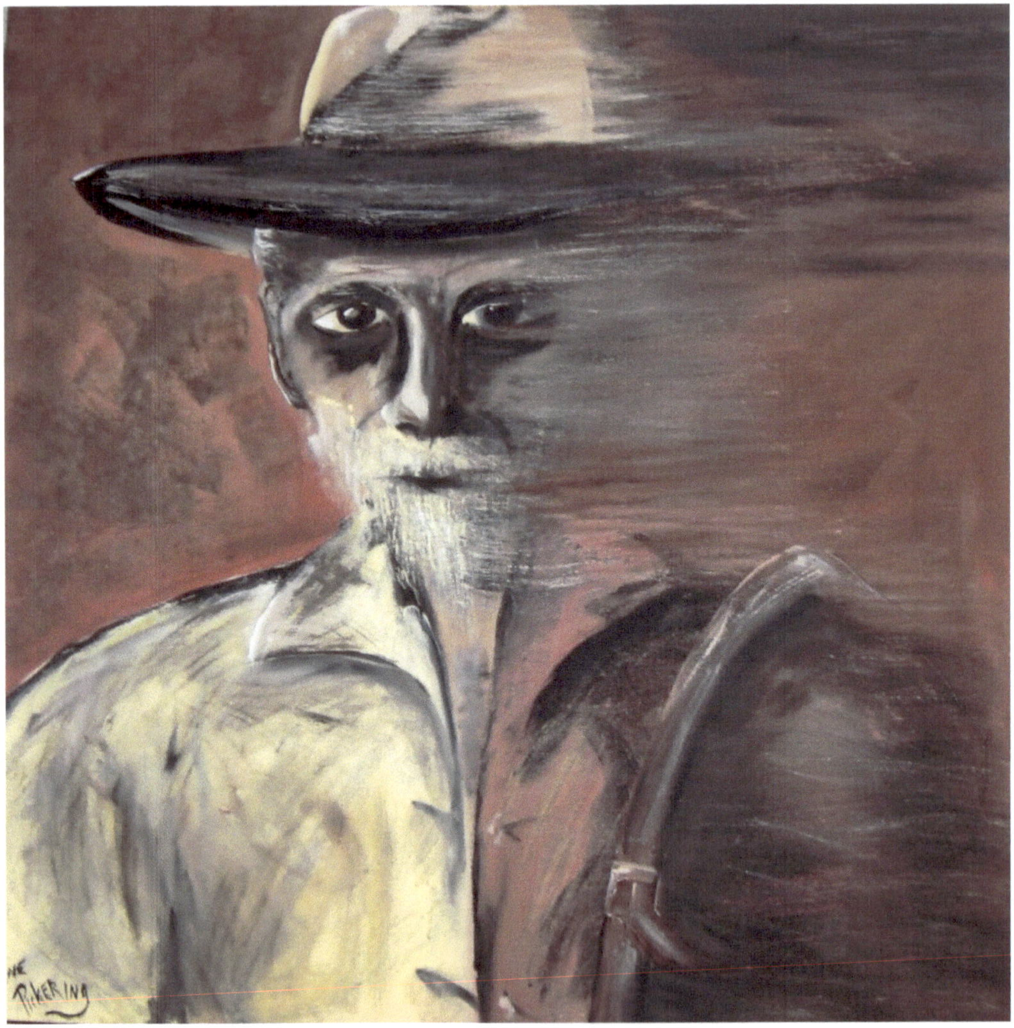
Pickering

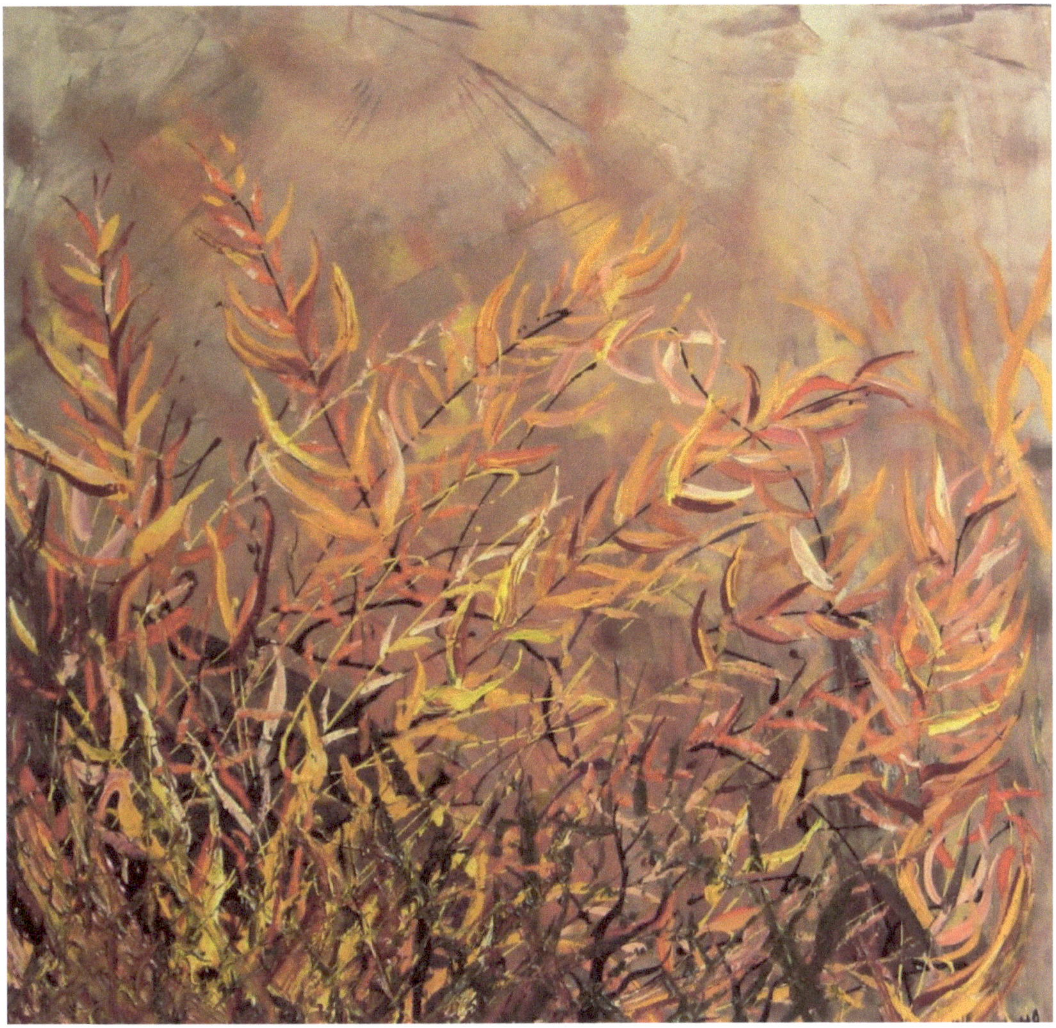

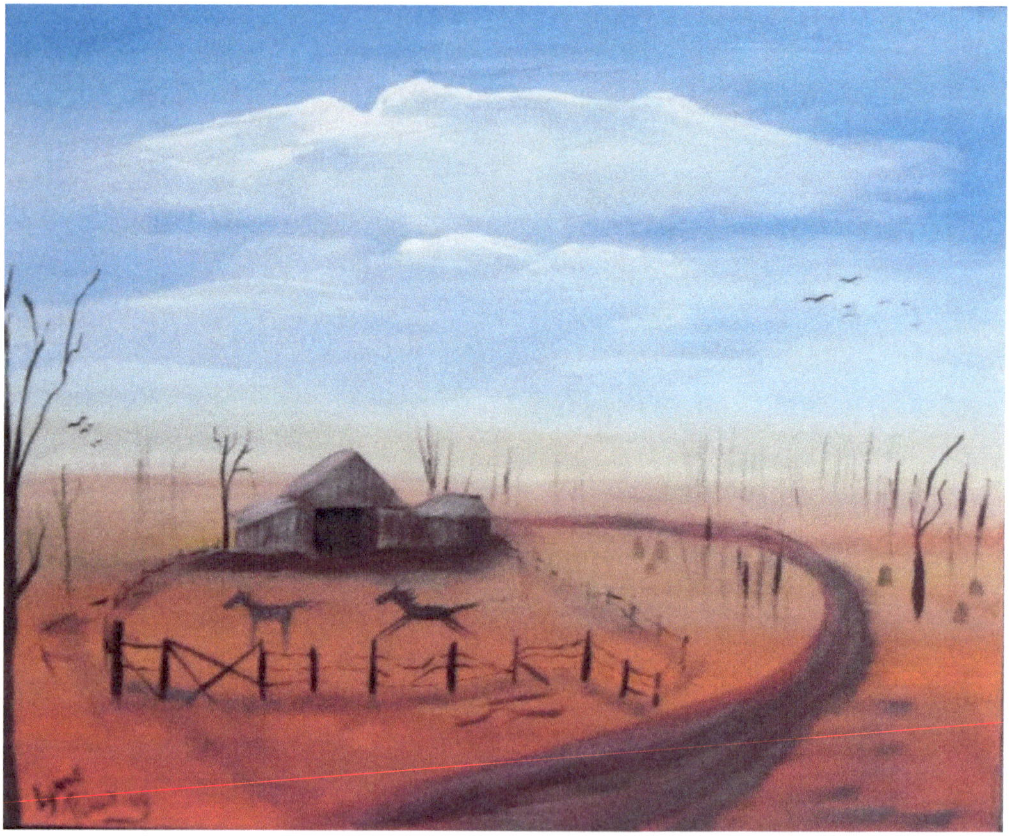

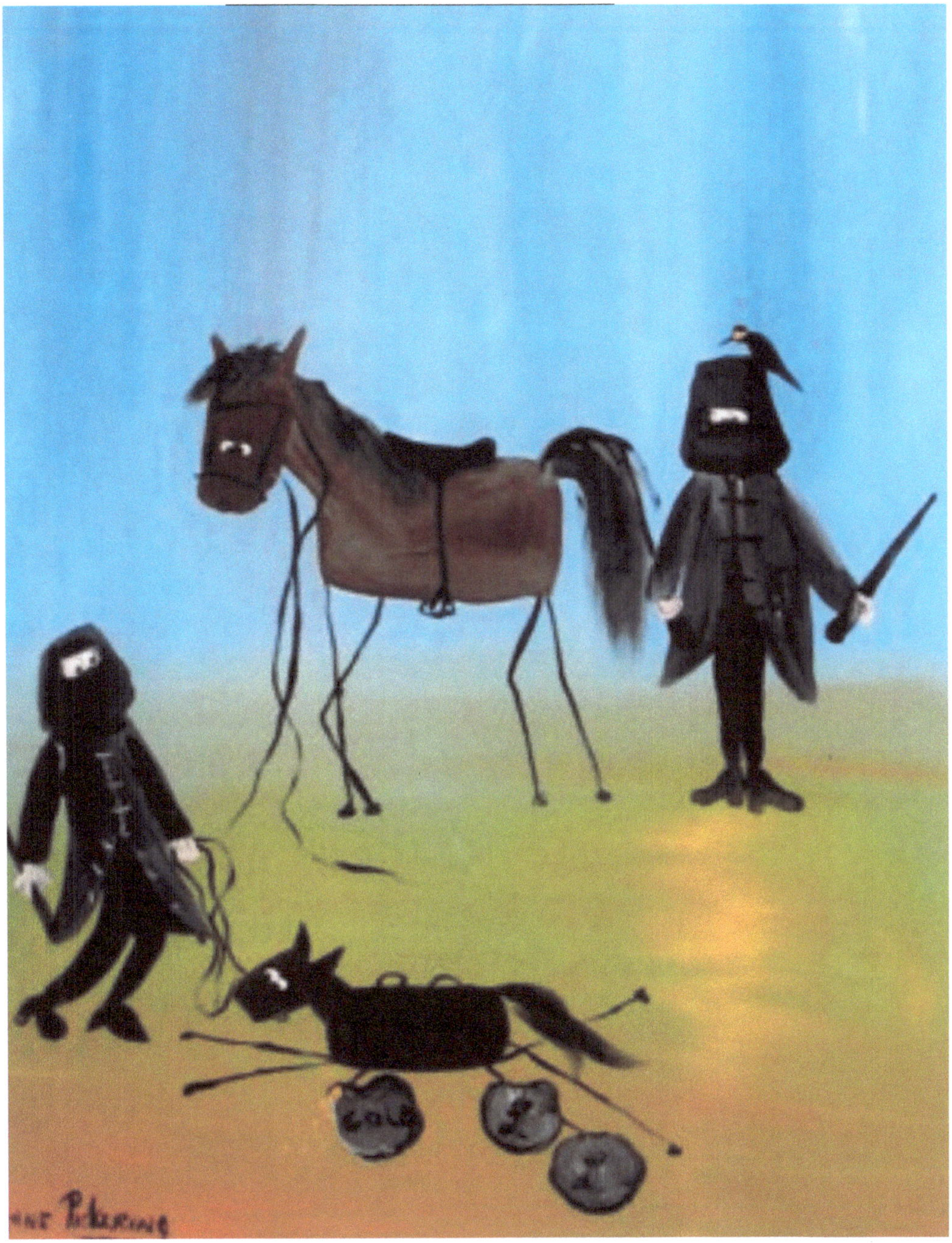
Pickering

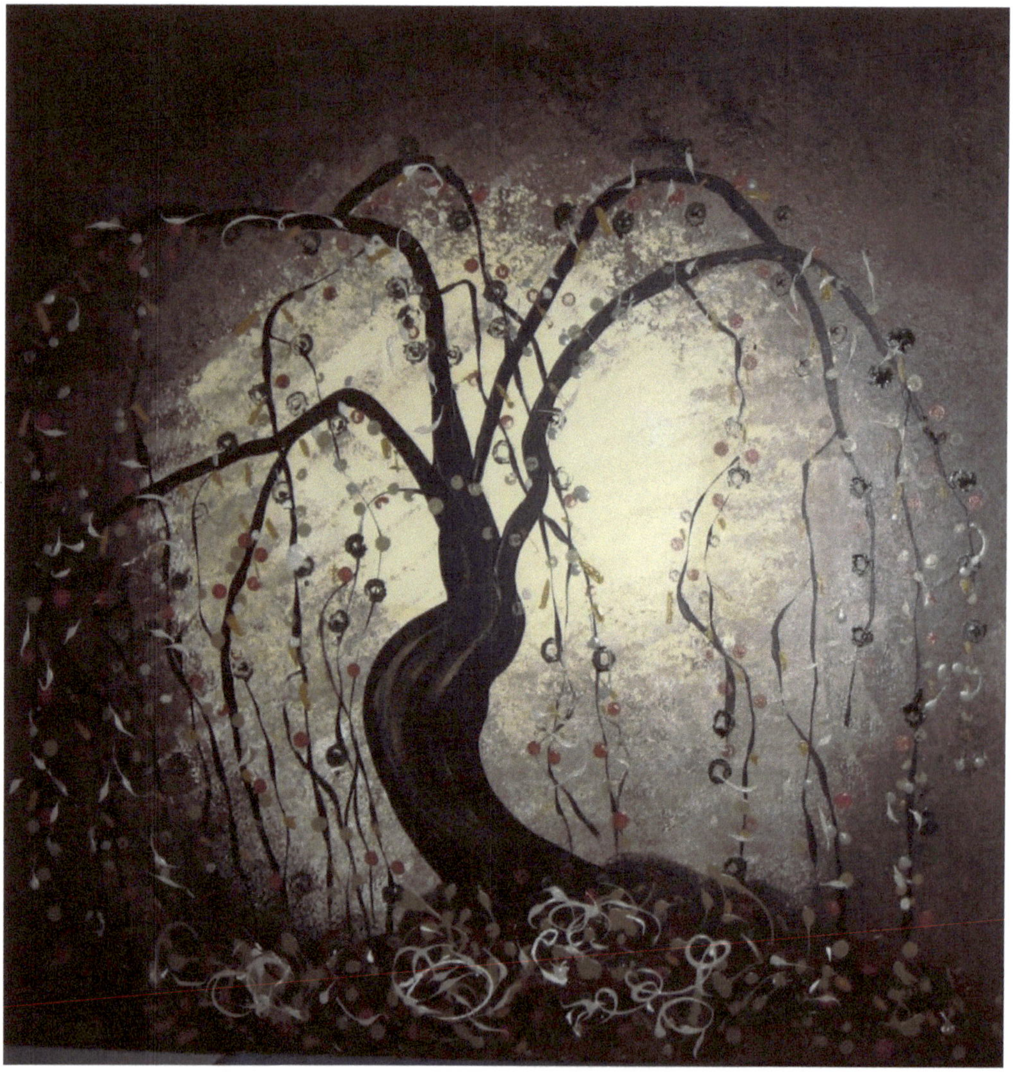

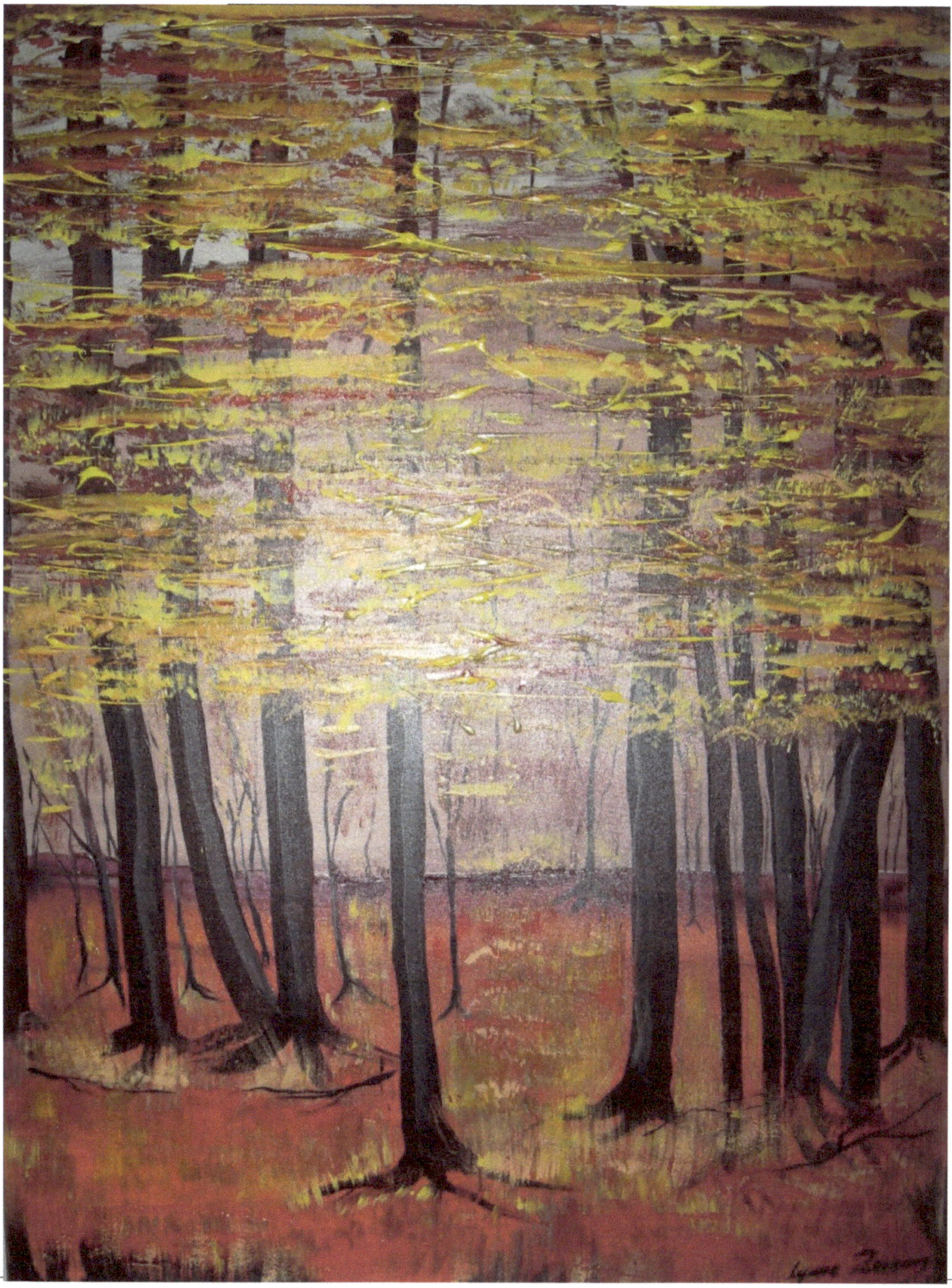

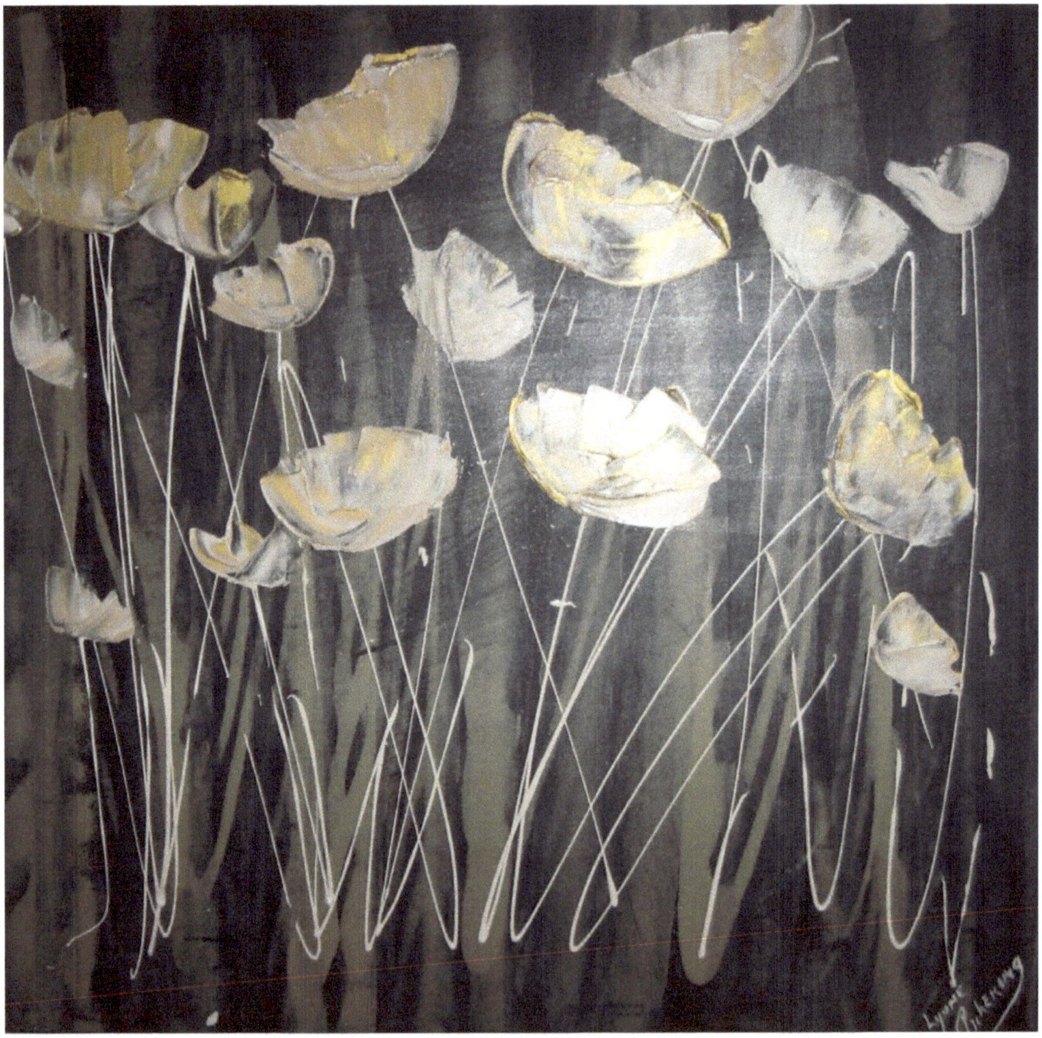

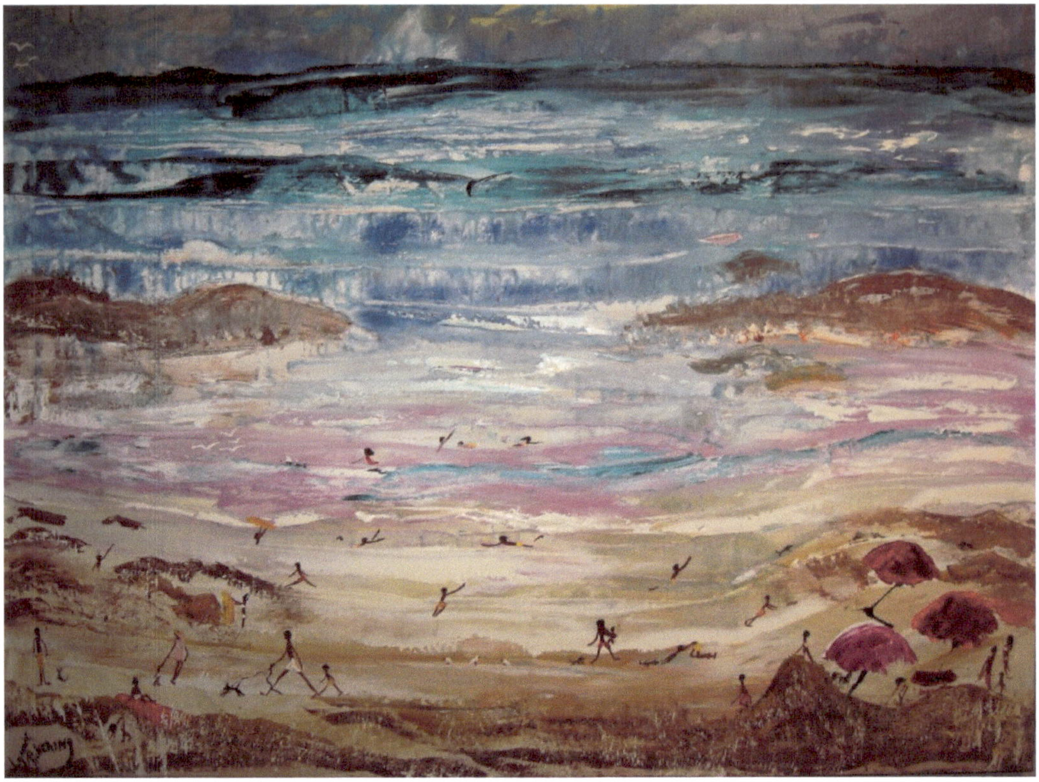

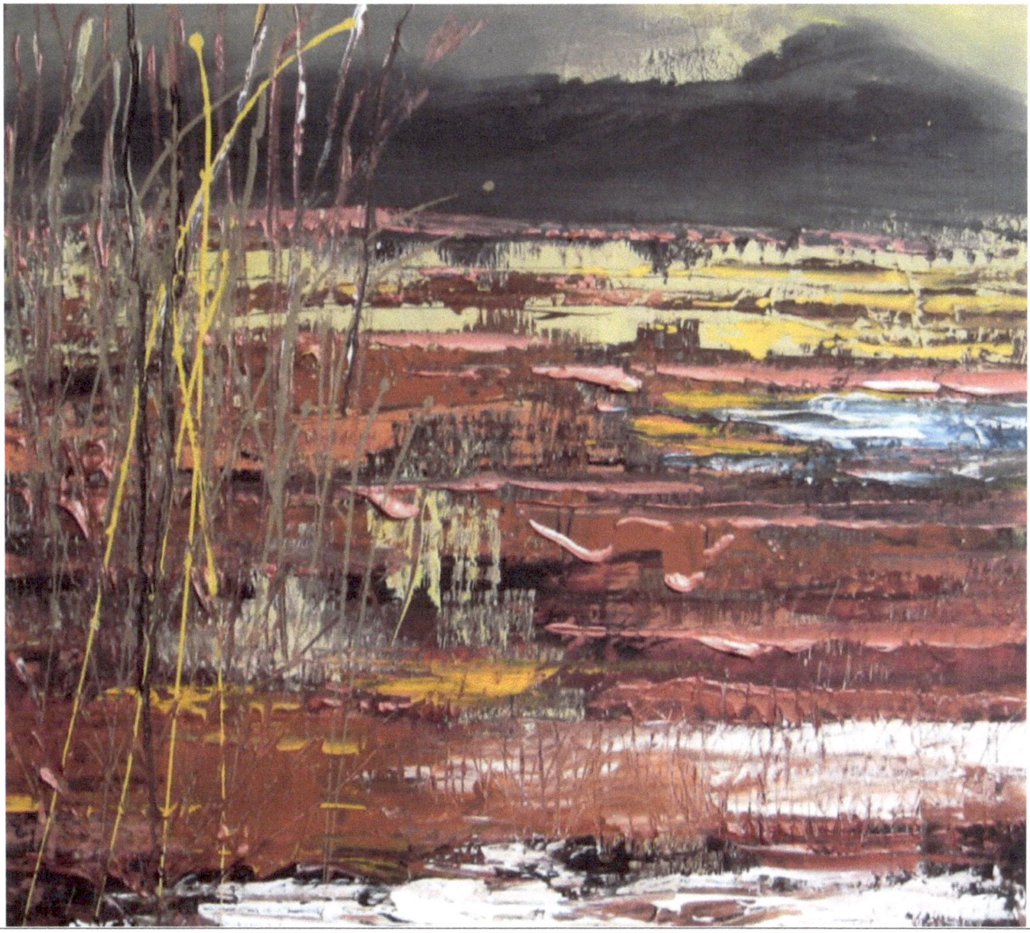

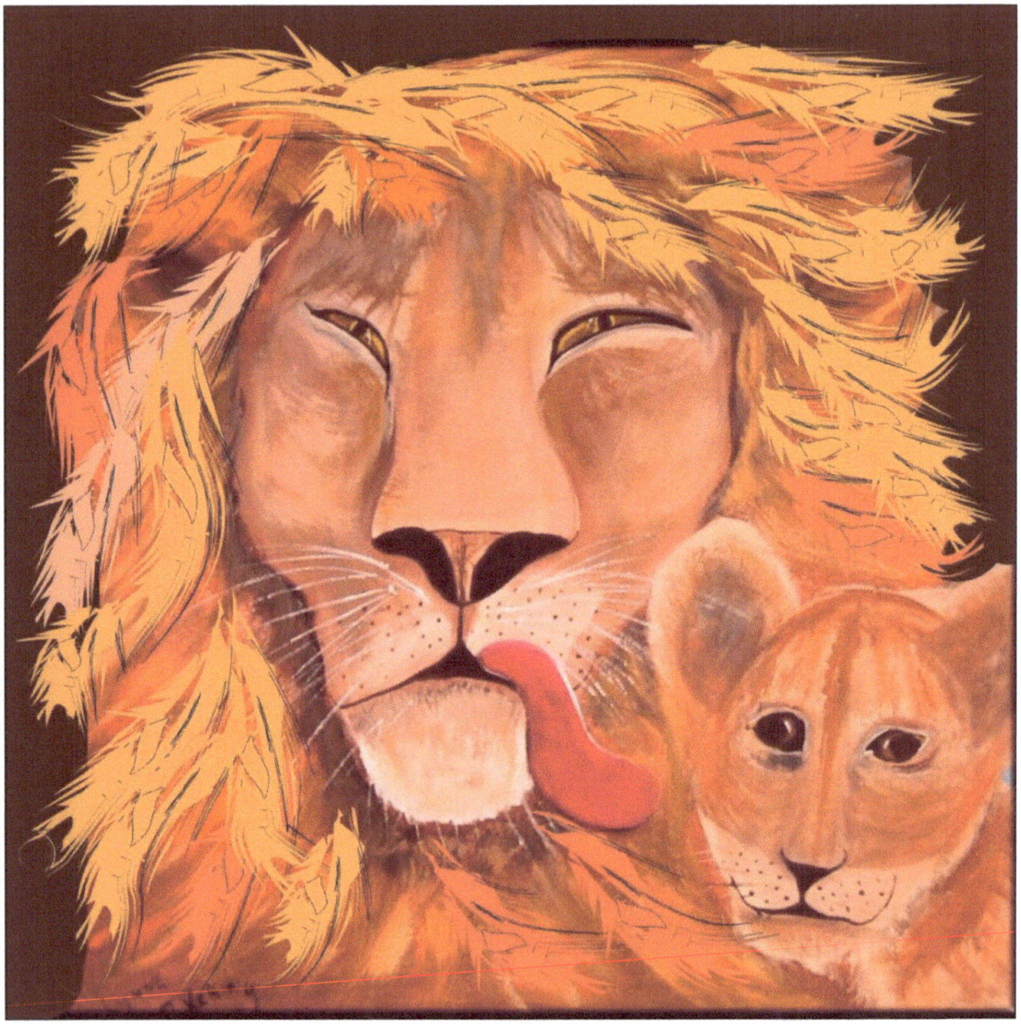

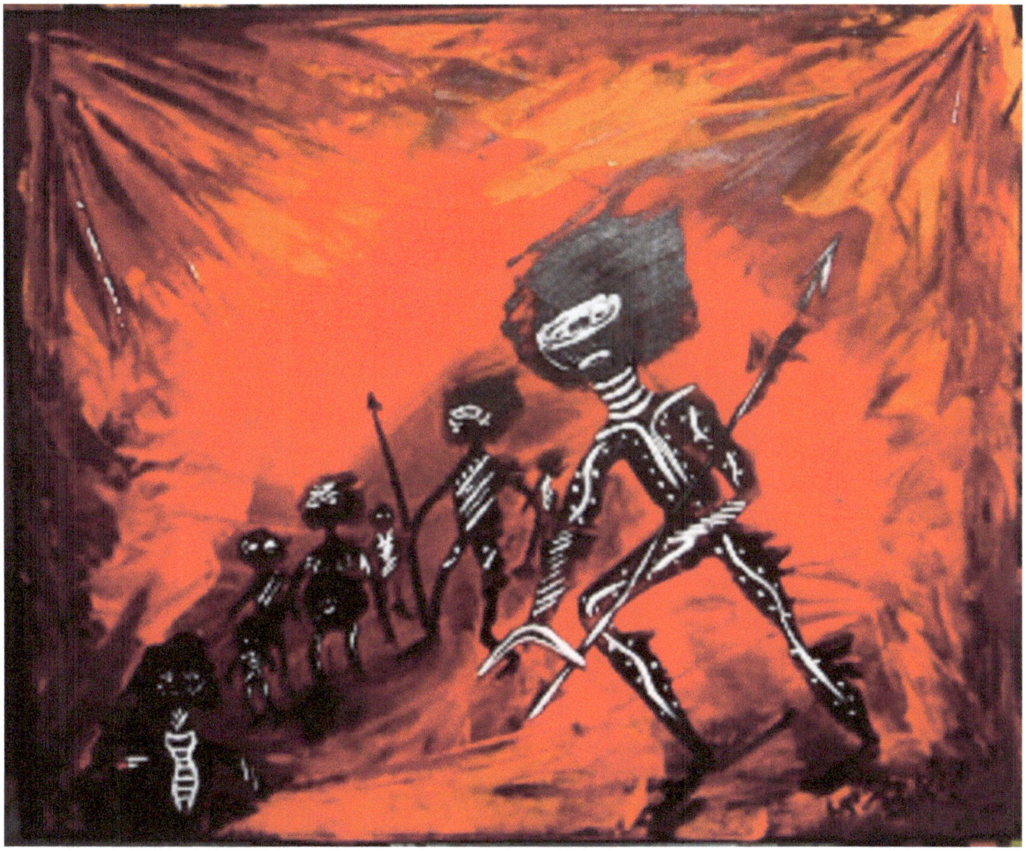

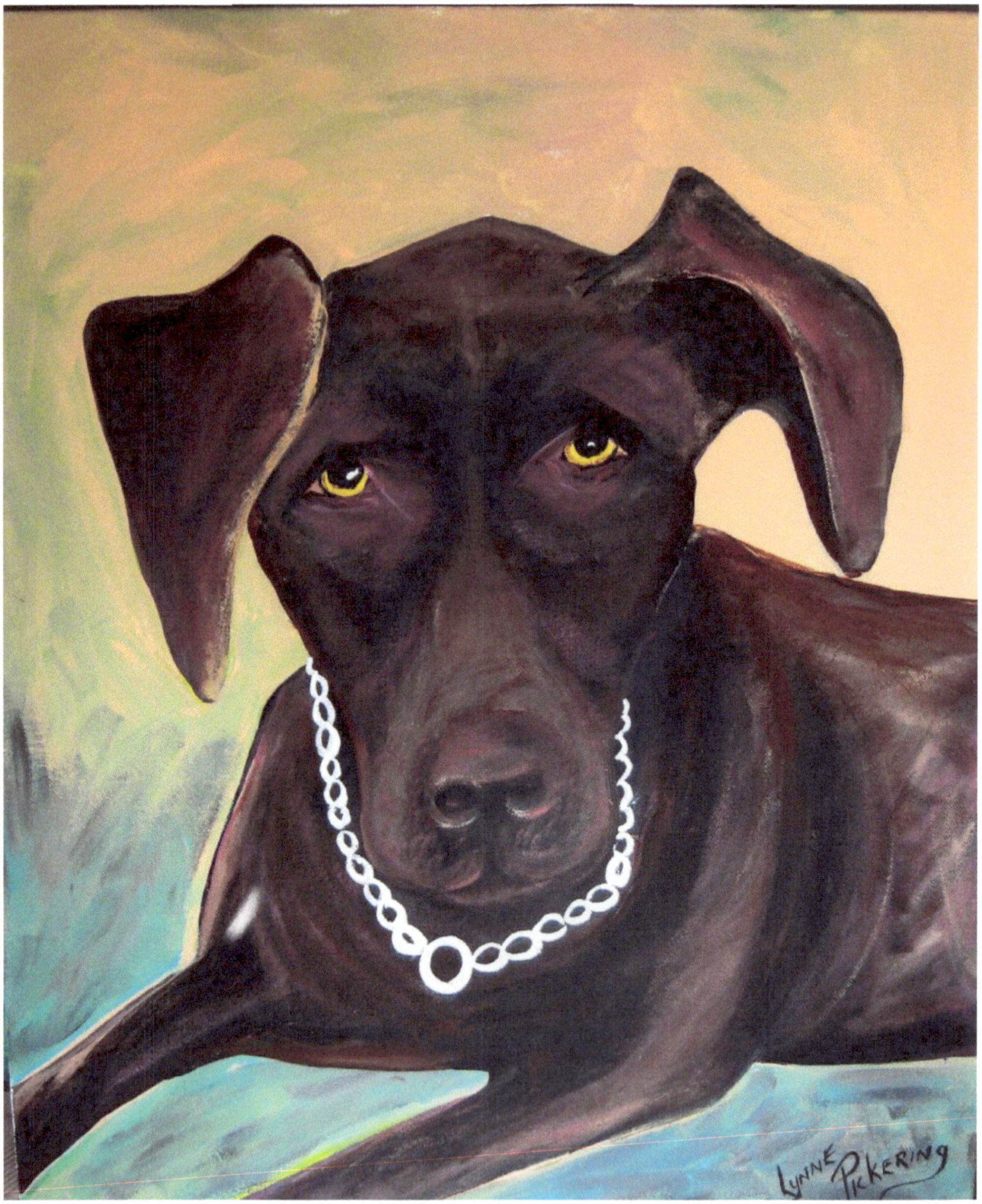
LYNNE PICKERING

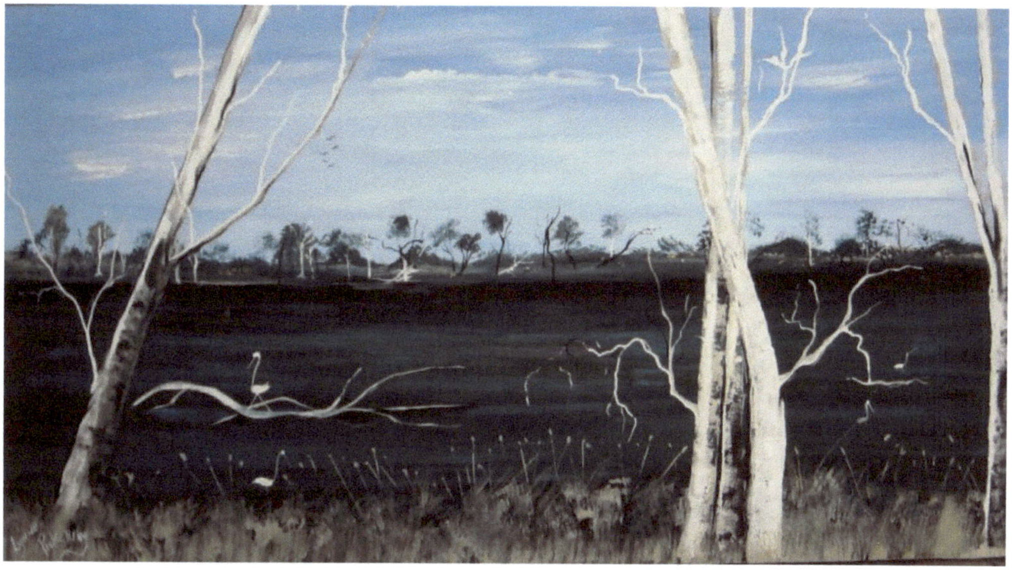

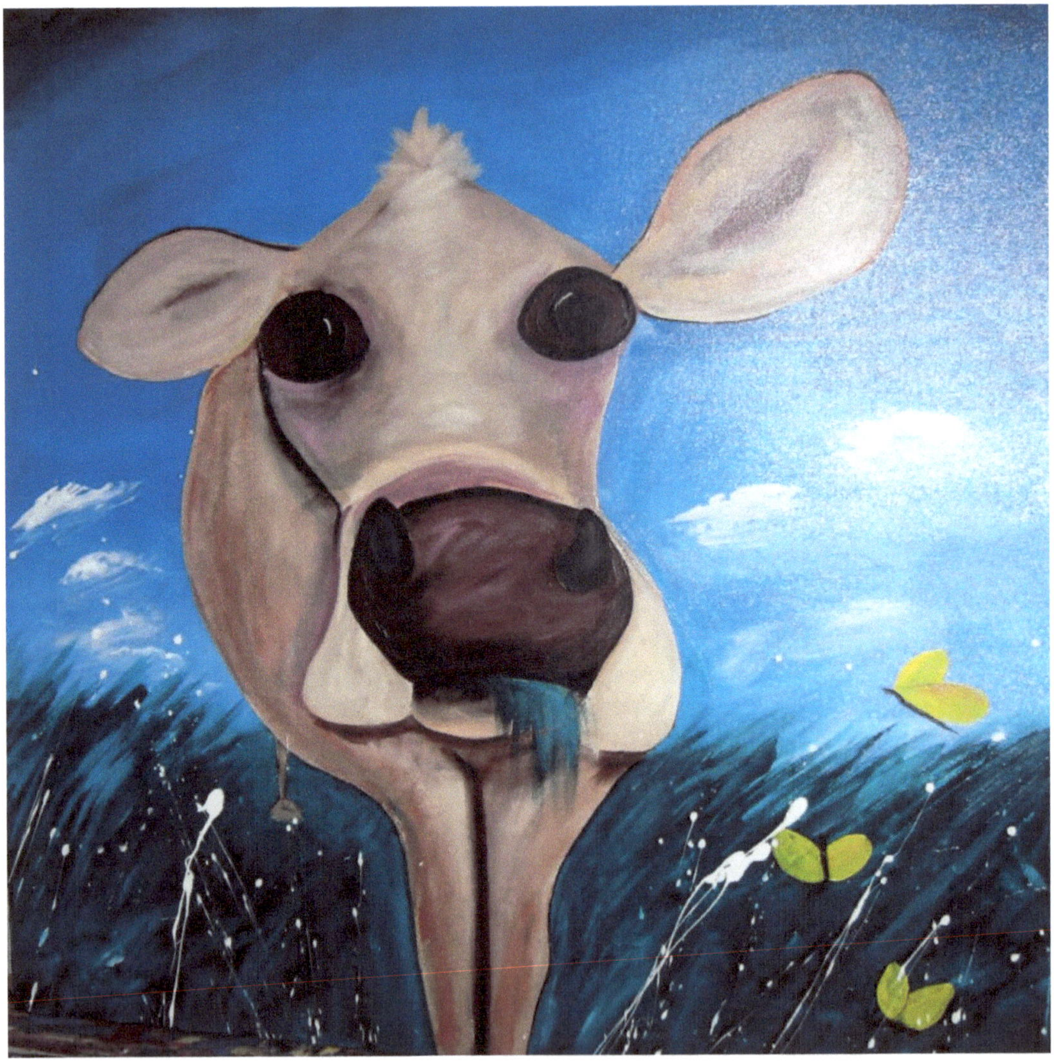

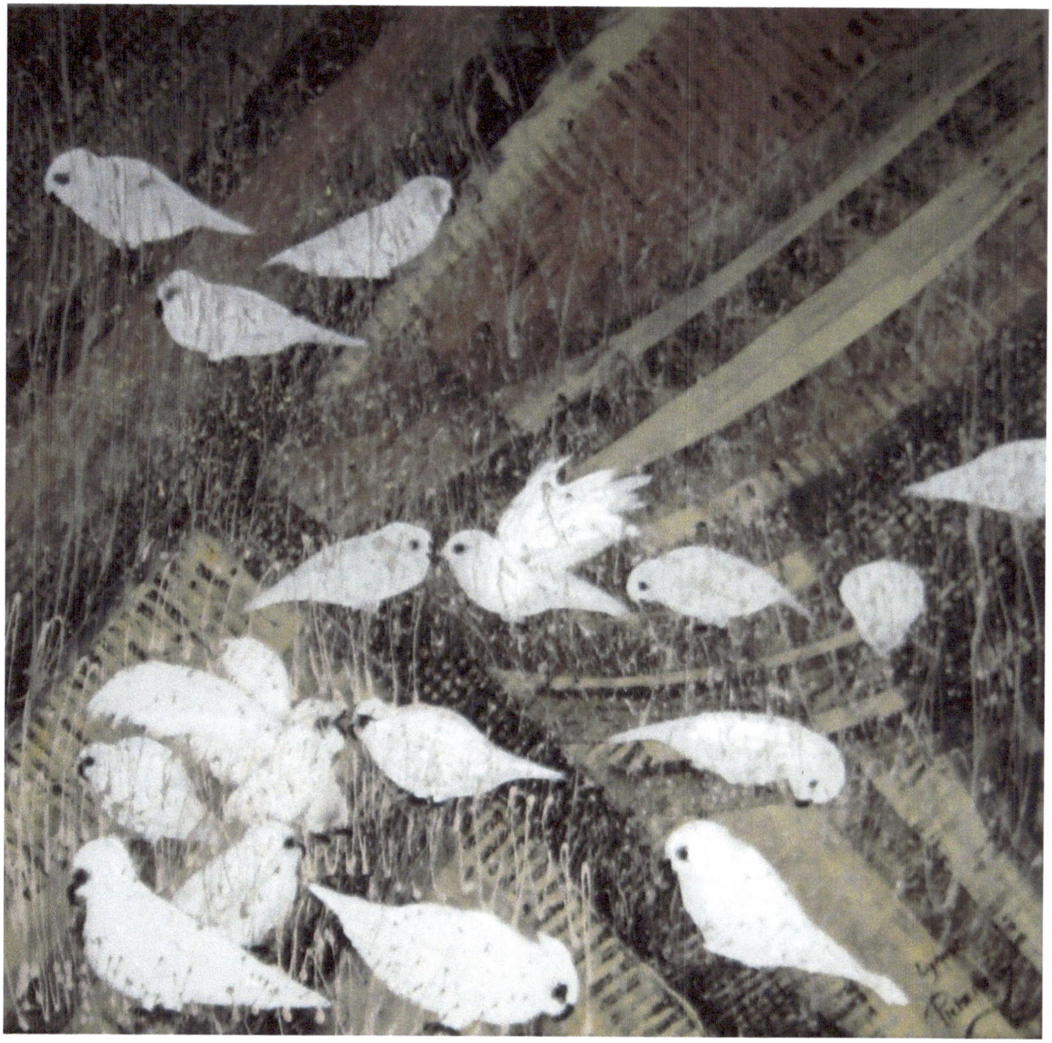

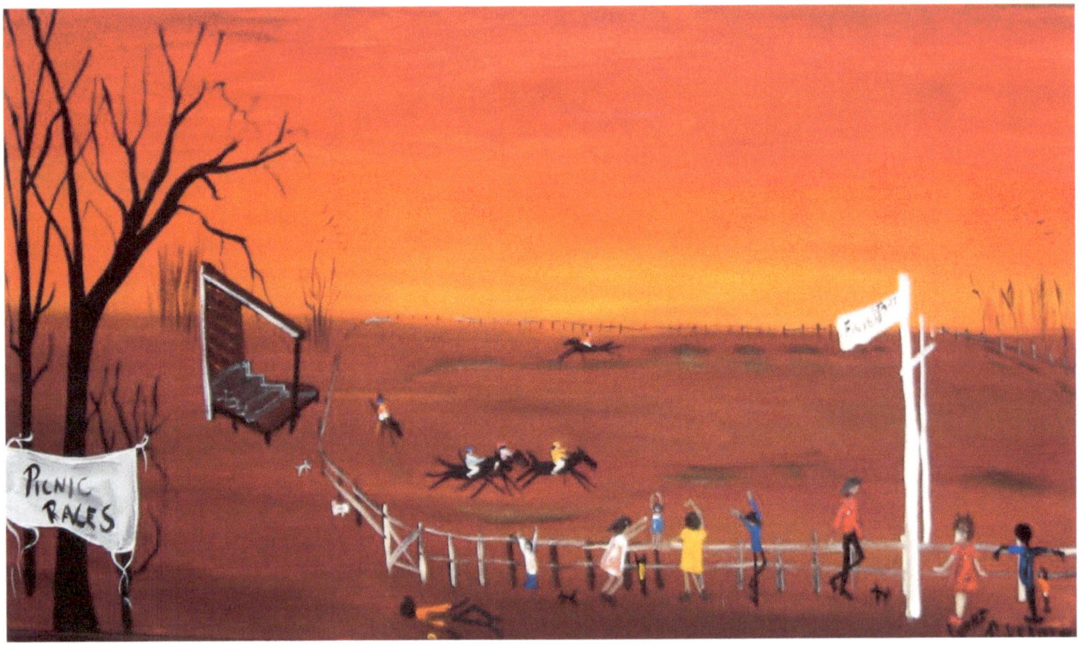
PICNIC
RACES

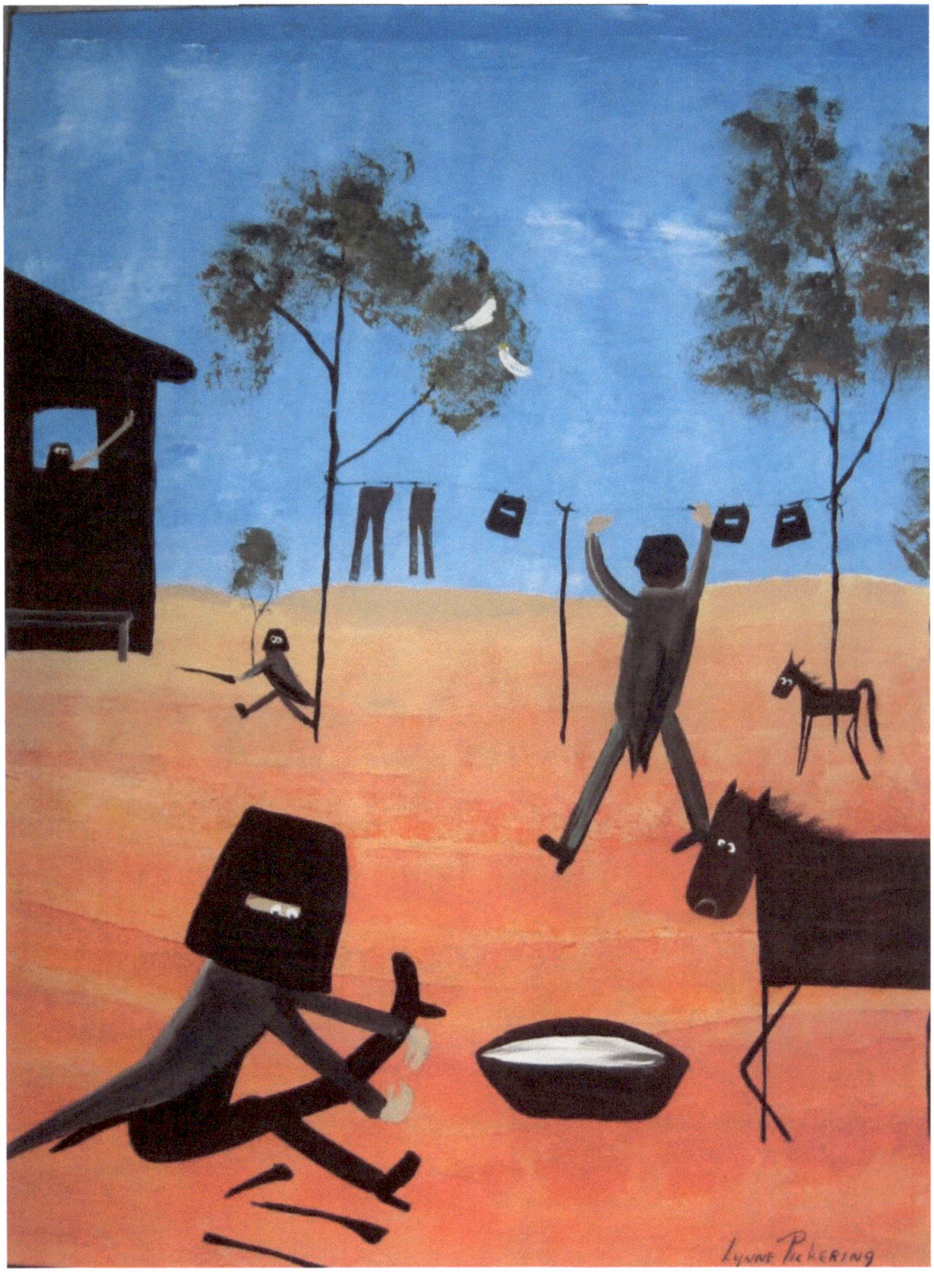
Lynne Pickering

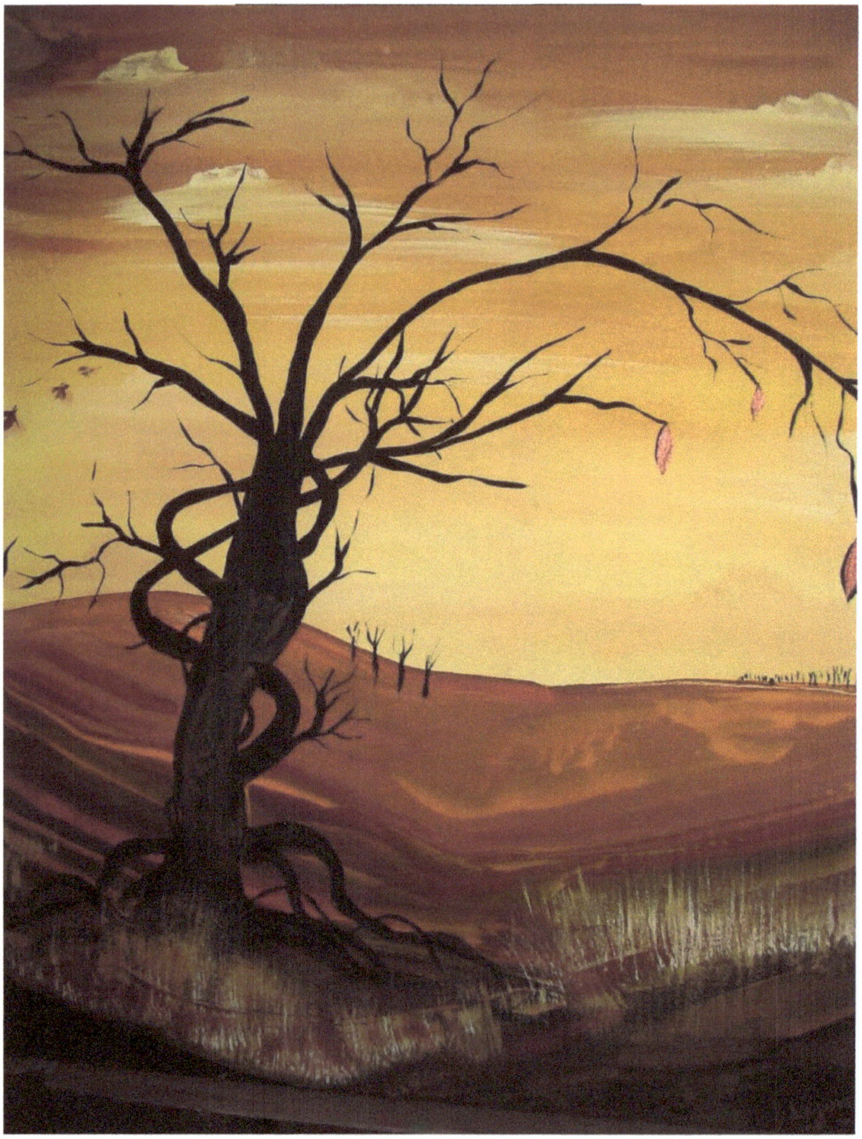

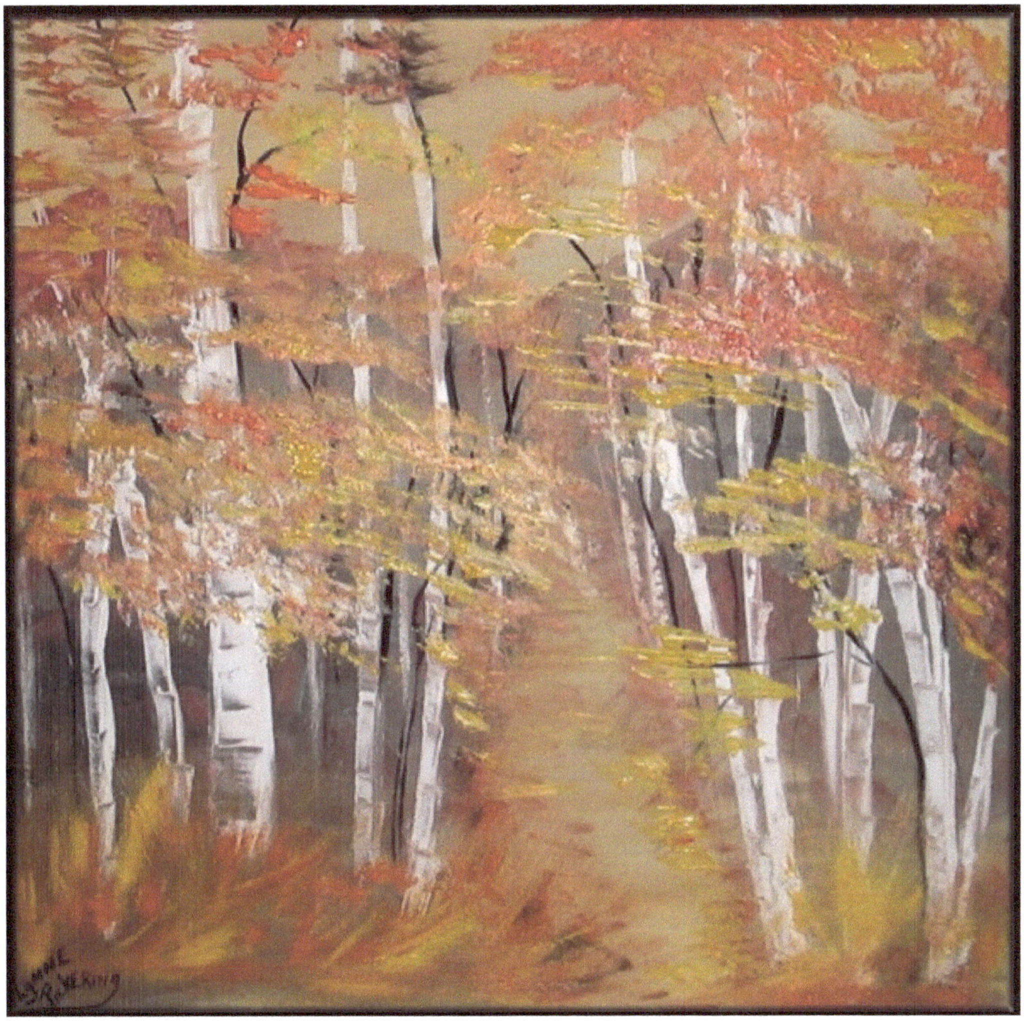

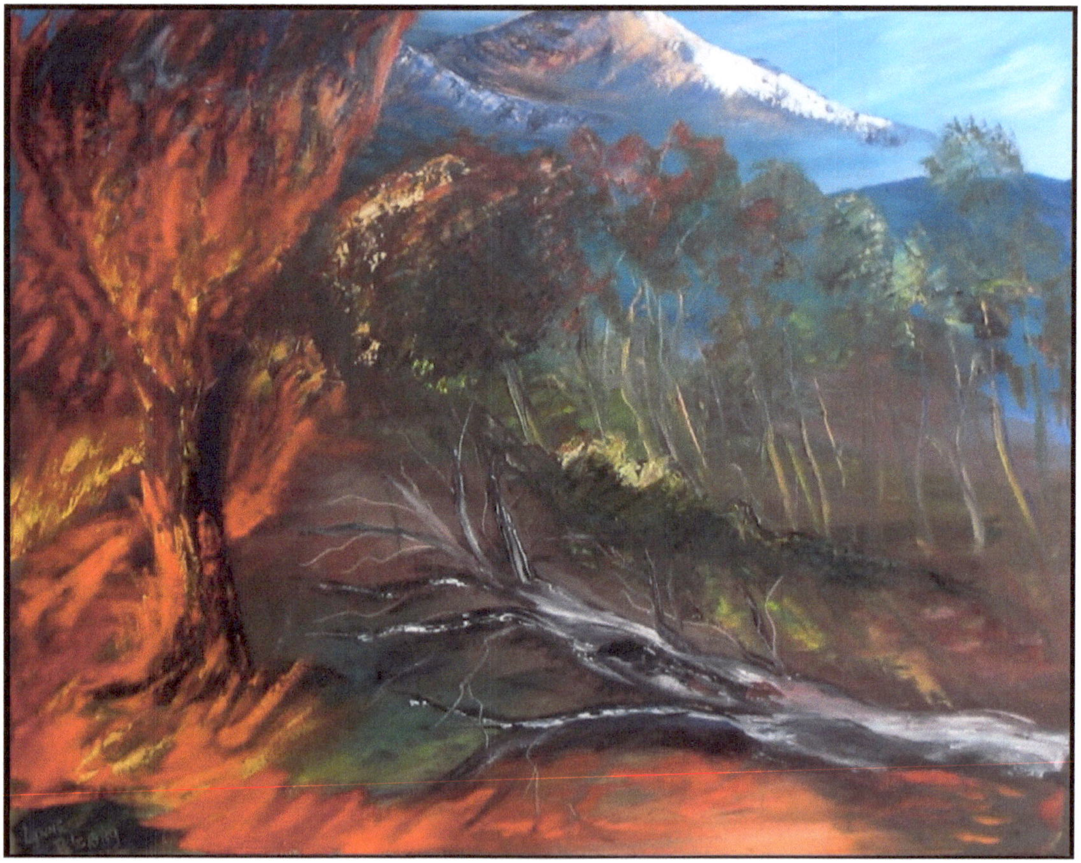

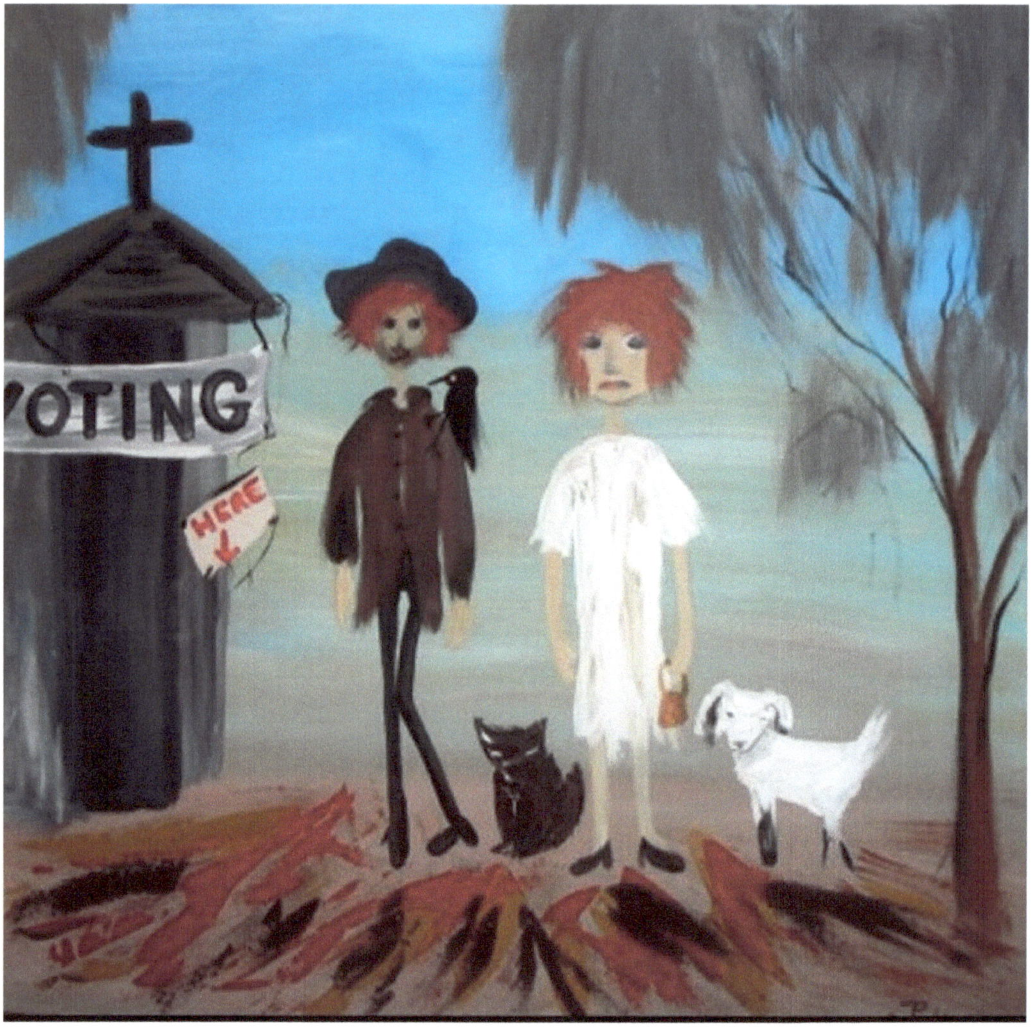
VOTING
HERE

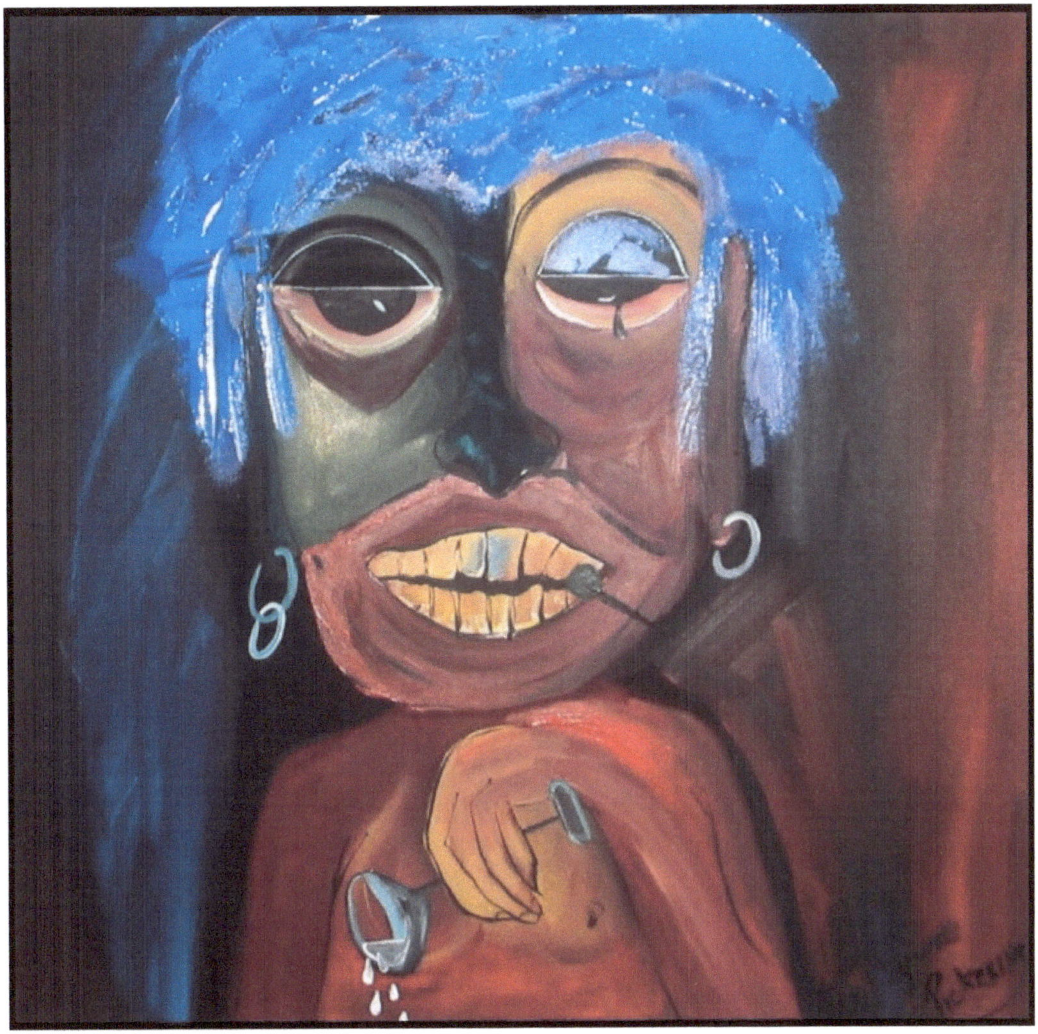

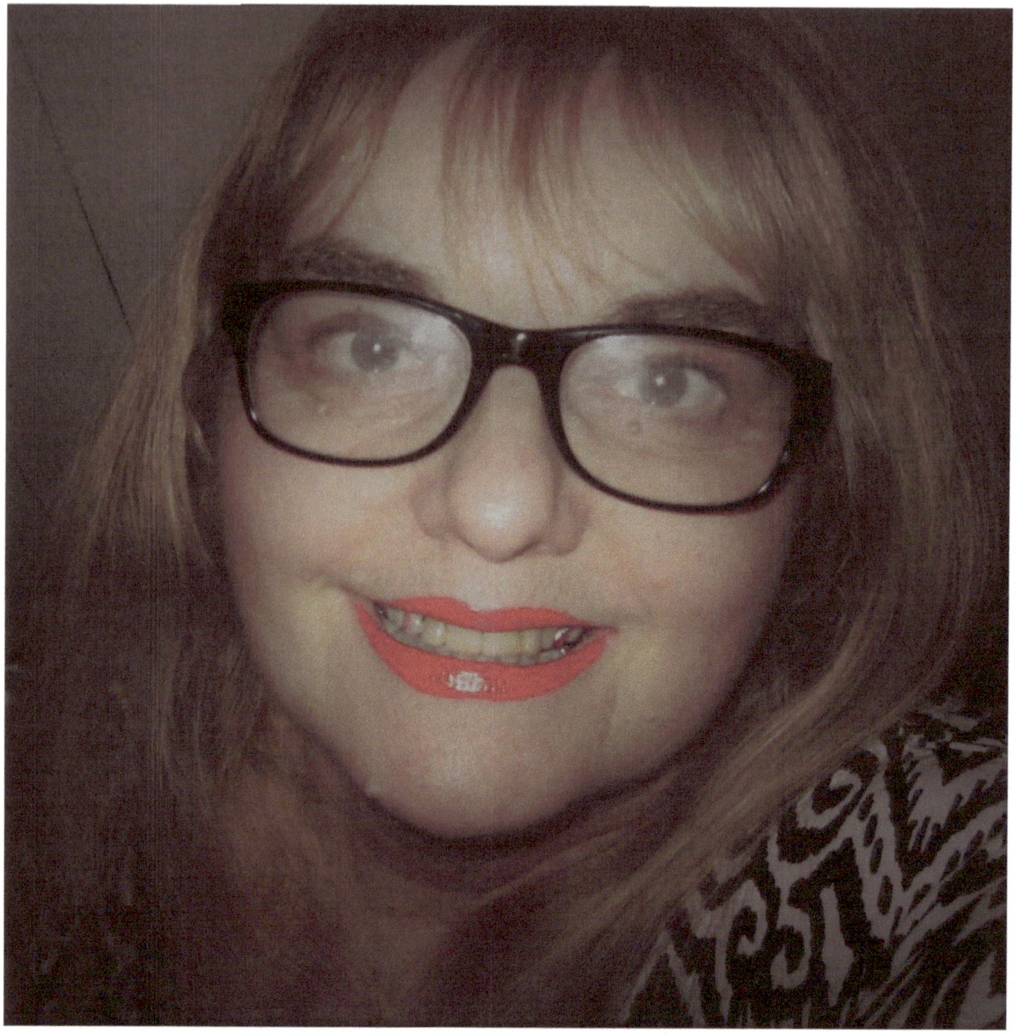

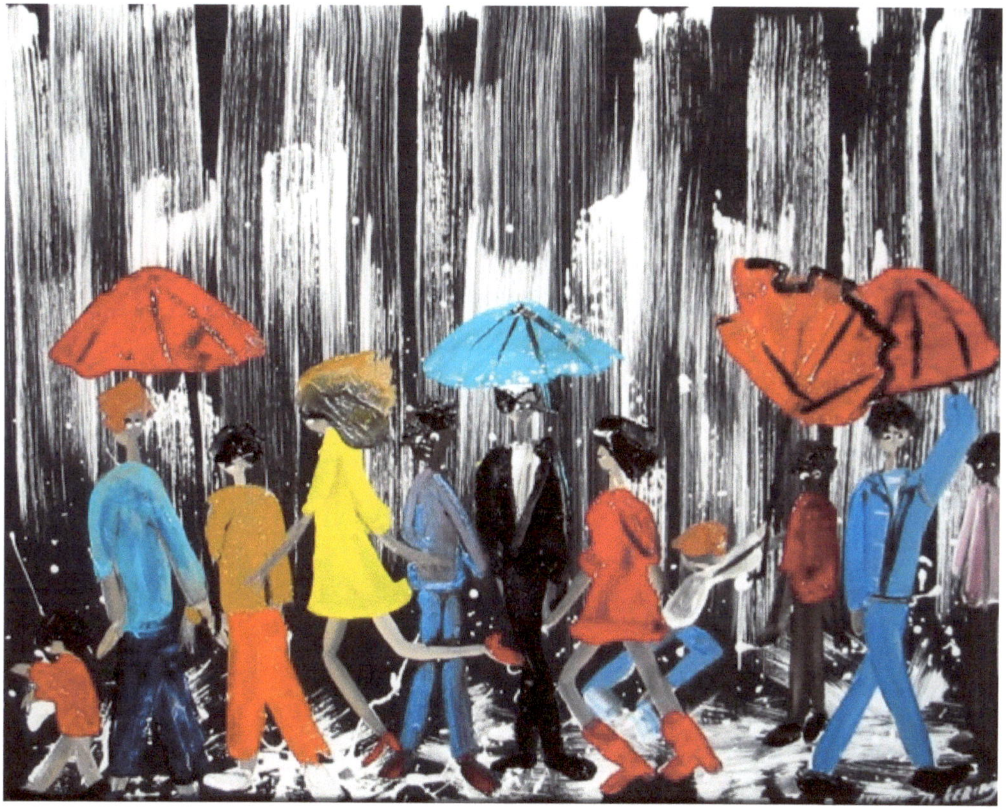

www.ingramcontent.com/pod-product-compliance
Lightning Source LLC
Chambersburg PA
CBHW051025180526
45172CB00002B/470
9781092791229